ikeCresc

THE 21ST CENTURY SUPERVISOR

Participant Workbook

BRAD HUMPHREY

JEFF STOKES

Jossey-Bass
Pfeiffer

SAN FRANCISCO

Printed in the United States of America

Published by

Jossey-Bass
Pfeiffer

350 Sansome Street, 5th Floor
San Francisco, California 94104-1342
(415) 433-1740; Fax (415) 433-0499
(800) 274-4434; Fax (800) 569-0443

Visit our website at: www.pfeiffer.com

Printing 10 9 8 7 6 5 4 3 2 1

This book is printed on acid-free, recycled stock that meets or exceeds the minimum GPO and
EPA requirements for recycled paper.

Contents

• •

• •

A Personal Word of Encouragement from the Authors

◆ ◆

We have had the pleasure of working with hundreds of organizations and thousands of supervisors over the past fifteen to twenty years. Our work has included on-the-job training in work areas, facilitating training and education classes, and conducting in-depth discussion groups. From this broad-based experience, we have deduced key characteristics of supervisors who have the *right stuff*. Supervisors with the right stuff

- Are confident without being cocky!
- Can laugh at themselves but take their jobs seriously.
- Work hard at making their employees better at their jobs.
- Are not afraid to ask questions, and are interested in learning—for a lifetime.
- Seek out challenging assignments that stretch their skills, without jeopardizing the safety of others or the satisfaction of customers.
- Focus on solving the problem at hand without passing on blame to others.
- Get as much (or more) excitement out of seeing their employees' success as they do from their own personal success.

Do the items on the this list seem almost impossible to achieve? If you have a burning desire to be the best supervisor possible in the twenty-first century, then this list of characteristics should excite you—even challenge you to be better.

The fact that you are going through the S-360 process is proof that you are serious about being the best supervisor possible. From our perspective, you have every reason to believe that you too will embrace and reflect the characteristics listed here.

• •

Good luck in your quest to be the best supervisor you are capable of being. Don't spend time comparing yourself to other supervisors. You have your own unique set of skills, interests, and strengths. Focus on what you can do to be the best you can be, and you will find many great days ahead.

Best of luck in all that you do!

Shawnee, Kansas
September 1999

BRAD HUMPHREY
JEFF STOKES

Chapter 1

● ●

How the Supervisor 360°
Skill Assessment Will Help You

Continuous improvement represents the never-ending pursuit of achieving better performance. Before any serious attempt is made to improve performance (whether personal, departmental, or corporate), it is vital to identify a *marker* that defines the current performance level. A marker establishes a *benchmark* against which all future performance can be measured and compared.

The Supervisor 360° Skill Assessment (S-360) establishes such a marker. The S-360 provides frontline leaders with a picture of their effectiveness in nine important skill areas at a particular point in time. Incorporating the leader's own assessment with an assessment provided by subordinates, peers, and managers (called *observers*), the S-360 generates an objective report that identifies skill competencies and deficiencies.

There are many instruments and assessments available today that define everything from behavioral tendencies to leadership effectiveness. Used appropriately, such assessments can be very helpful to individuals by identifying the areas in which they need improvement. The majority of such business instruments are general in scope, meant to be used by all authority levels. They are one-size-fits-all assessments.

In contrast, the S-360 is custom designed for one level of the workforce—the supervisor. This frontline leadership instrument is the result of over ten years of fieldwork with supervisors. We developed it to provide frontline leaders with a benchmark for identifying the effectiveness of their skills.

In our book *The 21st Century Supervisor*, we identified and discussed in detail the nine most important skills supervisors need in order to be successful in the twenty-first century. We showed how to make these skills part of the supervisor's leadership effort. The Supervisor 360° Skill Assessment and this workbook focus

● ●

on these same nine critical skills. Along with *The 21st Century Supervisor,* this assessment and workbook will assist you in identifying and strengthening your supervisory skills.

Benefits of the S-360

The nine skill areas assessed by the S-360 will be in great demand during the twenty-first century. The S-360 will help you

- Identify the skills you will need in the twenty-first century
- Gain insights into the expectations organizations will have for supervisors in the twenty-first century
- Determine your own effectiveness in the nine skill areas
- Assess your effectiveness as viewed by your employees, peers, and managers

The Participant Workbook

This participant workbook has been specifically designed for supervisors who have completed the S-360 assessment process. It will help you

- Understand what is expected of the twenty-first-century supervisor
- Comprehend what the S-360 measures
- Interpret the results of your S-360
- Identify your supervisory skills, both strengths and needs
- Refine your people skills
- Upgrade your technical skills
- Improve your administrative skills
- Develop your personal improvement plan
- Build greater accountability into your improvement effort

This workbook is divided into ten chapters. Here are brief introductory summaries of each chapter.

Chapter One provides an overview of the S-360, including the major components of the workbook, the benefits associated with the assessment, recommendations about which chapters to read before administering the S-360, and recommendations about selecting the observers who will also complete assessments.

Chapter Two gives a broad overview of the expectations awaiting many supervisors in the future. Some of the traditional roles and functions of supervisors are being reviewed and adjusted to meet these future demands and expectations. In this chapter, we offer a summary of our observations and experiences in our work with supervisors and other frontline leaders over the past fifteen years.

Chapter Three describes the skills that are assessed by the S-360. We selected these skills on the basis of a survey we conducted and in the light of what we learned as we assisted organizations in preparing frontline leaders for the challenges of the future. The nine skills are divided into three areas: people skills, technical skills, and administrative skills.

Chapter Four describes how to select the individuals who will be asked to complete the observer's version of the S-360. It also recommends specific steps for distributing and retrieving the S-360 so as to ensure that the formal assessment is sent to the appropriate individuals and returned for proper scoring.

Chapter Five presents the instructions for scoring the assessment. It also discusses how to interpret the S-360.

Chapter Six covers the importance of identifying the skill areas that need improving after interpreting the S-360, and it guides you in identifying those skill areas and preparing for further learning.

Chapters Seven, Eight, and Nine provide you with an initial opportunity to do some training in the three skill areas of people skills, technical skills, and administrative skills. The learning objectives addressed within these chapters are valid and important. In some instances you may find you require additional training time to ensure that you learn how to implement the skill being addressed. It may also be critical for you to expand your learning opportunity by taking training courses provided by your organization or such educational outlets as local colleges, universities, and commercial training companies.

Chapter Ten guides you in planning for your continued learning. A planning tool called the Personal Improvement Plan is provided so you can maintain a record of what you are committing to improve. We also provide some suggestions on how to build greater accountability into your learning.

The Suggested Resources section presents a selection of educational resources for additional reading and learning information.

It is recommended that you read the first four chapters of this workbook prior to completing the assessment. Becoming more familiar with the purpose and benefits of the S-360 will prepare you for the learning experience this assessment will offer you.

After you have read the first four chapters of this workbook, return to Chapter Four to consider in more detail how the S-360 will be administered and to follow the instructions.

It is also recommended that you act in conjunction with your immediate manager or a representative from your firm's Human Resource Department in carrying out the administrative steps. When selecting potential observers (the individuals who will be asked to complete an S-360 about you), it is important to select individuals who will be objective in their assessment effort. Having a manager or human resource associate assist you in the selection process ensures greater objectivity and avoids the possible favoritism that would skew the assessment results.

You should complete the *self* version of the assessment at the same time that the *observer* version is distributed to the individuals selected to complete it.

Personal Benefits from the S-360

Many people find it difficult to receive honest, objective feedback. Most leaders, including supervisors, prefer hearing only about the good things they are doing, not about the areas needing improvement. But without honest feedback a supervisor will never develop into a better leader of people and processes.

In the past many organizations neglected to ascertain their supervisors' performance. And even those that made the attempt often failed to give a supervisor in need of growth a significant improvement plan. Many companies did not directly guide the career growth of their frontline leaders.

If you are a supervisor who has never received consistent support from management, take heart! The S-360 will help put your development back on track. It will help you identify your effectiveness in the nine supervisory skills and then direct you toward improving the skills that will help you achieve greater supervisory results.

As the developers of the Supervisor 360° Skill Assessment, we are confident that you will find reason to be proud of your past performance. We are also sure that you will find areas within your supervision that need improving. Everyone does. Open your mind, and heart, to the feedback you will soon be receiving. Attempt to understand what your managers, peers, and employees are telling you. Compare their feedback to your own perspective on your supervisory effectiveness.

We are happy that you have chosen the S-360 to further your frontline leadership development. Do not let personal pride and past experience prevent you from learning more about your efforts as a frontline leader. Determine today to let the S-360 thrust you confidently into the twenty-first century, preparing you for greater roles and responsibilities as a supervisor.

Chapter 2

♦ ♦

Expectations of the 21st Century Supervisor

Many things taken for granted in traditional frontline leadership are changing for twenty-first-century supervisors. Although there are quite a few differences, including the greatly increased availability of advanced technology for the workplace, that have had a part in shaping the new role of the supervisor, we have identified a limited number of these changes that we believe are the most important ones to understand and act upon. These changes, which we will examine in this chapter, point to a need for a new style of leadership for the leader who has traditionally been called supervisor. The changes have certainly forced upon many supervisors a new set of expectations.

Contributions to a Changing Future

We believe there are four key contributors to the changes facing supervisors who wish to become leaders in the twenty-first century. First, the tangible impact made by the total quality movement has indeed arrived. What began in many organizations in the late 1970s and early 1980s has continued throughout the 1990s and will not slow down in the twenty-first century. Organizations that are serious about staying competitive (not to mention profitable) have all embraced some version of the quality movement that was thrust upon the United States during the late 1970s to early 1980s.

Ford Motor Company aired a television advertisement in the early 1980s that ended with a picture of a light bulb and, emblazoned across the bottom of the ad, the statement, "Quality is Job #1." This simple yet powerful phrase was soon adopted by organizations of every size and industry type. It seemed to capture what

♦ ♦

most companies wanted to achieve—whether or not they knew how to achieve it. In their search to become the perfect organization, many companies began a long journey of never-ending training in such areas as quality principles, problem solving, and team-based management.

Interestingly, for many organizations, the improvements have come. Although the improvements may have taken longer than expected, most organizations can point to better delivery of product or service than they could ten or twenty years ago.

How has the quality movement affected supervisors? The theory behind the quality process is to push the accountability for arriving at better results to the frontline employee. Thus many companies have invested a great amount of time and money in training and education programs over the past thirty years for their frontline employees. Who has had to learn right along with the frontline employee? You guessed it, the frontline leader—the supervisor!

Sadly, frontline employees often received the training and education prior to the supervisors. This gave many supervisors a bad taste in their mouths about the quality movement. Some even felt as though the quality movement was designed to get rid of their job function. Though this was not the purpose of the quality movement, many supervisors did find themselves without a job or in a job that could no longer be handled in the way they were used to working.

The supervisor's role was not the only role affected, and this leads us to a second contributor to the changes facing twenty-first-century supervisors. History will most certainly show that the 1980s and 1990s were a period of accelerated corporate mergers, buyouts, and alliances. Unfortunately, such corporate change often resulted in layoffs, especially among the middle-management ranks.

As corporate downsizing continues, the roles and responsibilities of the middle manager have remained even though the middle managers themselves are gone. In many organizations those roles and responsibilities have been acquired by the supervisors. For example, traditional supervisors were not always expected to develop an annual budget for their work areas. Although they may have possessed and benefited from an understanding of the financial side of their departments, the actual development and monitoring of the yearly budget was executed by a department manager.

Another example of tasks once usually performed by department managers is resource management. It was more often this manager than the supervisor who identified needed resources such as technology, equipment, information, and people. Though the traditional supervisor may have been asked for input on such needs, the department manager was the one who checked viable sources for needed information or technology. It was the manager who secured the services of a consulting group or proposed the purchase of new equipment to senior managers. Now this activity too has fallen to supervisors as more and more managers are displaced from the organization.

A third contributor to the changes facing supervisors is the issue of profitability. Often it is perceived that an organization will sell its soul to make a profit. The past decade has witnessed merger after merger and companies selling off unprofitable divisions. All this just so a predetermined profit margin can be reached and an organization's stock price can satisfy the stockholders.

Although obtaining profits has always been at the core of for-profit organizations, corporate leaders are increasingly dependent for those profits on those who make most of the day-to-day decisions—especially the supervisor at the front lines. The quality movement often uncovered unnecessary costs and waste that might range from 25 to 40 percent of a company's total sales. (See the Suggested Resources for reading resources on quality, specifically the books by W. Edwards Deming and by Joseph Juran.) There was so much poor management of processes and people in some companies that as much as forty cents of every dollar earned was simply wasted.

When such waste was identified, organizations looked for any means possible to reduce it and in that way build more profits into the products or services. Because supervisors are at the front lines, they have become critical players in this drive to reduce costs and waste and to reach greater profitability. This makes it essential that supervisors understand such terms as profitability, cost-benefit analysis, return on investment, and per unit costing. Decisions made by supervisors at the front lines have to incorporate more financial information and understanding than has ever been expected in the past.

A final contributor to the changes facing supervisors is the reality of speed in the workplace. Speed is the result of completing needed work with a minimum of interruptions and obstacles. Elimination of these time wasters allows for a maximum effort to be made to meet the expectations of the customer.

As competition continues to escalate for every industry, it is vital for supervisors to identify, assess, and remove every roadblock that prevents their employees from meeting shorter delivery times than ever before. Truly, the speed with which an organization can fulfill each customer's needs will greatly influence whether that customer's business can be retained.

Each of the four contributors we have identified here demands a new kind of supervision. Gone are the days when supervisors were paid mainly to perform carefully defined tasks—to distribute paychecks, collect timecards, carry a wrench, or write up bad employees. Some of these traditional functions may continue, but greater expectations are in place for twenty-first-century supervisors.

Functions of the 21st Century Supervisor

The changes described in the previous section have forced a new set of expectations on the role of supervisor. In our years of working with supervisors, we have observed two common functions of traditional supervision. One function demanded supervisors to be hands-on, technical leaders. They were expected to be just as involved with performing the work as frontline employees. As they moved from employee to employee, they were expected to do whatever it took to get the work completed—including doing the work themselves.

The second function positioned supervisors more as administrative assistants to department managers. These supervisors were supposed to do only what the manager instructed them to do. In most situations they were not expected to think "outside the box" or to solve problems (unless perhaps to consider how to implement an order passed down from the boss).

Although there was certainly no shame in these two functions of supervision, both fall short of allowing supervisors to reach their potential. Greater expectations will be placed on twenty-first-century supervisors. We project that future supervisors will be expected to

1. Unify a more diverse workforce
2. Possess greater communication, documentation, and presentation skills
3. Become teacher, coach, and facilitator
4. Make greater use of technology
5. Drive performance success through process thinking
6. Possess greater financial understanding

Let's review the significance of these six expectations.

1. *Unify a more diverse workforce.* The U.S. workforce continues to become more culturally mixed. Just as diverse, however, are individuals' work ethics, job expectations, education, and experience. Supervisors have the unique challenge of bringing all this diversity together and forging the differences into a unified working unit. The need for a more unified workforce is behind many organizations' efforts to drive greater teamwork. Supervisors will find themselves coaching their teams to produce greater performance results in a more profitable manner.

2. *Possess greater communication, documentation, and presentation skills.* With greater diversity comes the need for supervisors to be more effective communicators than ever. In some sections of the United States, this could require being bilingual, but the ability to dialogue with different age groups, listen before responding, and confront poor performers without starting a war is the major communication

requirement. Faced with higher expectations for quality, future supervisors will also be required to capture quality control efforts on paper. Supervisors will be responsible for producing reports, analysis overviews, strategic plans, and responses to customer requests—all in writing! Because supervisors will be expected to have more business knowledge of their work areas, they will also be expected to make presentations to upper management. And then they will have to teach presentation skills to their employees, because those individuals will be making presentations about problem-solving efforts.

3. *Become teacher, coach, and facilitator.* Most supervisors will find themselves expected to fill the roles of teacher, coach, and facilitator. They will be expected (and needed) to raise the job skills, process knowledge, and decision-making abilities of their employees. Although in-house trainers and outside training consultants will still be used, the essential and ongoing day-to-day training and education will be driven by the supervisor. Coaching demands that supervisors spend time studying their people, noticing development needs and then coaching (instructing) employees on the improvements. With greater emphasis on teamwork, supervisors will initially take on the facilitator role, leading meetings and working to involve their employees in taking ownership of their work areas and processes. The true measure of a supervisor will be his or her ability to lead employees through making decisions and solving problems without causing the employees to feel they have been manipulated, strong-armed, or coaxed into taking action. As facilitators, supervisors will guide their employees to understand their situations and needs, and will provide the resources for employees to make the best decisions.

4. *Make greater use of technology.* There is no escaping the fact that the never-ending improvement of computer power has changed the way supervisors supervise—forever. Information is power, and that power is delivered through greater use of a computer. Information that took days, weeks, or months to acquire only ten years ago is now available in seconds. Supervisors will not have to be program analysts or hardware consultants, but having that knowledge will not hurt them either. Supervisors will be expected to know the software resources available to them and to ensure that such information is made available to their workforce. Combining this expectation with that of being teacher and coach, supervisors will be expected to raise the technical skills of their employees. Computers are a prime component of speed in the workplace, and supervisors must take advantage of available technology to improve their work areas.

5. *Drive performance success through process thinking.* Quality gurus such as W. Edwards Deming and Joseph Juran have impressed upon business leaders that as much as 85 percent of the problems in the workplace result from process problems. Process is *how* something works. Quality and statistical process control (SPC) teach that improving the work process (how something is completed) is

the most certain path to better end results. Supervisors will be expected to drive constant improvements in work processes. This will require them to view most activities in the workplace as a constant series of processes. Approaching the workplace as a series of processes enables supervisors to reduce the negative impact made by some individual personalities and opinions. Perceiving activities as processes allows greater objectivity and measurement. Process thinking also empowers supervisors to forego short-term corrective action in order to search for long-term solutions that improve performance and produce correspondingly long-term positive results.

6. *Possess greater financial understanding.* Organizations are constantly looking for ways to tighten their financial belts. Decisions made by supervisors are increasingly important to the overall financial security of any company. Supervisors will be expected to consider the financial ramifications prior to making any final decision. When purchasing equipment or hiring additional employees, supervisors will be required to show a cost analysis of their current situation and to calculate the probable return on investment. Without the financial understanding that such methods produce, supervisors will be unlikely to make the best decisions and to win the support of upper management.

These expectations are real. They are not only expected—they are fast becoming job requirements for many supervisors. The nine skills identified in this workbook address these expectations. Improving in the nine skills (the subject of the next chapter) will make you a more valuable asset to your organization, and strengthen your career success.

Chapter 3

• •

What the Supervisor 360° Skill Assessment Measures

The Supervisor 360° Skill Assessment (S-360) is an assessment to identify the skill competency of supervisors, or anyone who is involved with leadership at the front lines. The assessment, or evaluation, provides information about how well the supervisor is performing on nine specific skills important to supervision.

The Nine Supervisor Skills

Over the past fifteen years and more, as we mentioned earlier, we have worked with over five thousand supervisors. This work has often consisted of coaching and training supervisors in professional leadership techniques. In this process, we have used various leadership assessments to confirm or identify leadership strengths and weaknesses. We focused on identifying specific needs that could be addressed through education, training, or personal coaching.

To gain greater insight into assisting supervisors in their professional development, we began a search to identify the skills supervisors need in order to be more successful. Because of the many changes taking place in most industries (see Chapter Two of this workbook), we found that many organizations now need supervisors with a different set of skills than traditional supervisors have possessed.

As described in *The 21st Century Supervisor,* we identified nine skills that supervisors will need in order to execute the changing functions that so many of them will face in the future. Once we identified these nine skills, we set out to design an assessment that would provide an objective, accurate measurement of a supervisor's skill proficiency. This effort resulted in the Supervisor 360° Skill Assessment.

• •

The nine specific skills (fully discussed in *The 21st Century Supervisor*) fall into three skill areas: people skills, technical skills, and administrative skills. The following list offers core descriptions of these skills.

People Skills

Communication skills involve the ability to listen attentively to others and to interact with them in a manner that is constructive and effective. These skills require supervisors to understand the different communication styles practiced by others. They also require supervisors to be able to perform formal communication tasks, such as making presentations.

Team skills involve the ability to create a unified approach to work by engaging individuals to work together cooperatively. These skills require supervisors to lead and facilitate team meetings and to assist employees to move through the four recognized stages of team growth (forming, storming, norming, and performing).

Coaching skills involve the ability to assist employees in identifying their improvement opportunities and then in making the needed changes in their work effort. These skills require an ability to confront and counsel employees as well as to teach and instruct them. Effective coaching embraces solid communication skills and team skills.

Technical Skills

Business analysis skills involve the ability to identify costs associated with performance and make better decisions using important business information. These skills require supervisors to be more knowledgeable about operating costs, including the costs associated with mistakes. Supervisors with these skills are capable of developing budgets and monitoring performance indicators for their work areas.

Continuous improvement skills involve the ability to maintain a never-ending pursuit of performance improvement. These skills require a working knowledge of the techniques and disciplines of quality, continuous improvement, and problem solving. The supervisor must be able to recognize performance variances, determine the impact these variances have upon performance, and know how to reduce these variances with cost-effective solutions.

Computer skills involve the ability to operate a computer and use available software resources for the development of presentations, reports, financial analysis, graphs, and so forth. These skills must be exercised daily as the supervisor makes use of the information gained through the computer system to improve decision-making and resource management efforts.

Administrative Skills

Project management skills involve the ability to identify long-term objectives and develop the action plans necessary to accomplish those objectives. These skills require being able to create a vision of the future for a work area and to communicate that vision clearly to others. Supervisors must also be capable of tracking performance in order to calculate completion dates and identify the resources needed to complete projects on time.

Writing skills involve the ability to communicate in writing so that others receive clear, accurate messages. These skills require supervisors to develop written reports, write letters and e-mail messages, and effectively complete company-required paperwork. Although perhaps the most hated skill area for most supervisors, these skills are also important ones for extending and promoting a supervisor's career.

Resource management skills involve the ability to search for and identify resources that supervisors and their employees need to perform their jobs. These skills require networking with others, building relationships with industry experts, and building a base of knowledge about such resources as consultants, suppliers, and physical tools and equipment. These skills also require understanding and maintaining budgets and knowing how to prepare for future needs.

Let's also look more closely at the three skill areas into which the nine skills identified here fall. People skills are pivotal to supervisory success because (1) the employee base continues to grow more diverse, (2) team-based management is becoming the norm at more organizations, and (3) many employees who are new to the workforce need personal monitoring and coaching.

Technical skills are being redefined. Traditionally, having good technical skills implied having experience on machinery or equipment. Although such technical skills remain important, the term has evolved to include a broader range of skills. The ability to make good decisions by thoroughly analyzing the business (financial) perspective is increasingly important for supervisors. As companies

press forward to meet greater customer demand and schedules, supervisors must be educated and proficient at continuous improvement practices. And there is no excuse for supervisors in the future not to have computer knowledge and skills. The *tent* called technical skills is expanding to include all these varied skill sets.

Finally, perhaps our most interesting discovery is the need of most organizations to have frontline leaders take on a greater portion of the firm's administrative duties. Project management, writing, and resource management were skills typically expected from managers (who may have had more education or professional training than the average supervisor). Of the three skill areas, administrative skills may be the newest to supervisors.

Why You Should Measure the Nine Skills

Can you be professionally successful without being highly effective in all nine skills? Yes. Performing the nine skills simply adequately will give you job security in most industries and organizations for the next few years. But as the pressure grows on your company to deliver higher profits, you will be required to elevate your department's productivity. That will require you to be highly effective in each of the nine skills measured by the assessment. You may already work in an industry that requires highly effective use of the nine skills.

Supervisors who possess and use the nine skills consistently will

- Be more effective in their job performance (and in their manager's eyes)
- Create a positive environment in which frontline workers can excel
- Lead by example, and encourage others to do likewise
- Work proactively instead of reactively, thereby reducing job stress
- Maximize their department's productivity
- Raise the skill and performance levels of their staff
- Elevate the morale of the entire department
- Lower interdepartmental barriers
- Open up advancement opportunities not normally available to frontline leaders

Assessment Reliability

The Supervisor 360° Skill Assessment would not be valuable to you if it were not accurate and reliable. We have tested this assessment to ensure it meets important professional standards. These tests reveal the assessment to be

- *Internally reliable:* The five specific questions pertaining to each of the nine skills correlate well with separate individual ratings for each of the skills.
- *Test-retest reliable:* Observers who complete the assessment once and then complete it again within a time period too short for the supervisor's skills to have changed receive scores on the test and retest that are consistent with one another.
- *Independent skills reliable:* The nine skills measure independent talents; no two are closely correlated to one another.

Assessment Sense-Ability and Predictability

The results of the S-360 have *sense-ability*, that is, they make sense to the individuals who read them. This is important because, clearly, if you (or any other supervisor) cannot make sense of your results, you will not learn what you should about the effectiveness of your supervisory skills. The results also have *predictability*, that is, they reflect your current level of effectiveness with the assessed skills in a way that allows others to predict, to a degree, your effectiveness in the near future (unless you have increased your skills in the meantime by embarking on further development and improvement).

OK, So What Do I Do Now?

If you are serious, almost anxious, to grow as a supervisor—then move on ahead. Good leaders, from company presidents to frontline supervisors, realize that honest, objective feedback is critical to self-improvement. Making positive use of the feedback from this assessment will put you in the driver's seat on the road to achieving greater personal development.

Consider the dashboard of your car. It has many gauges you use to monitor your car's performance. Let the Supervisor 360° Skill Assessment be your personal dashboard. Allow the results to give you insights into your supervisory performance. Don't react negatively to scores that may be lower than you like. Just as important, don't become lackadaisical about skills with a high rating.

Using this assessment appropriately will enable you to take greater control of your own destiny. View your improvement efforts as a long-term experience, a journey into continuous self-improvement. Stay focused on efforts that reaffirm your commitment to being the best supervisor you can be—and allow the feedback from others to guide you. You control your own destiny!

Chapter 4

• •

How to Use the
Supervisor 360° Skill Assessment

The Supervisor 360° Skill Assessment provides feedback on your supervisory skills. It does not measure behavior, personality, leadership style, or intelligence. It is a diagnostic tool that identifies your personal opportunities for improvement and will help you prioritize your professional development activities. The S-360 also serves as your road map for performance improvement.

The Supervisor 360° Skill Assessment consists of two components: a *self* assessment, which you fill out, and an *observer* assessment, which is filled out by multiple observers who are familiar with your work: your direct reports, your peers, your manager. The observer assessment generates feedback on your effectiveness in using the nine critical supervisory skills identified in the previous chapter. Therefore the individuals who are selected as observers must be closely familiar with the skills you use in your role as a frontline leader.

At a minimum, your observers should include your direct reports and your immediate manager. Because additional valuable information can be obtained from your peers and key personnel in other departments, distributing the survey to them may benefit you greatly. The survey is designed to prevent forced responses from unknowledgeable observers, which could bias the results. Individuals who are not in a position to judge your effectiveness on a particular skill can select a *no knowledge* response.

Distributing and Collecting the Assessments

We recommend that your senior manager or a representative from your firm's Human Resource Department assist you in distributing and collecting the S-360 for observers or that they conduct the following process for you. To use the

• •

observer and self assessment instruments for maximum effectiveness, follow these steps:

Step 1   Determine how many direct reports you would like to obtain feedback from—the more, the better. We recommend that five to seven direct reports (subordinates), three to five peers, and your manager or supervisor all complete the observer assessment. (As you choose individuals, plan your selections so you avoid ending up with a group that is on the whole either overly positive or overly negative. Try to find a balance.)

Step 2   Put your name and the relationship of the observer to yourself on the front cover of each observer assessment.

Step 3   Write your name and the address to which the assessment should be returned on the summary scoring sheet.

Step 4   Write a brief note thanking your observers for their sincere, honest feedback. Give them specific instructions about the name of the person or office that should receive the completed S-360 and by what date it should be returned. You and your observers should maintain confidentiality by avoiding discussion of the assessment with anyone, as this will ensure more objective feedback.

Step 5   Complete your own self assessment instrument. Do this before you read the observers' responses. You and your observers respond to exactly the same statements covering your effectiveness on the nine skills. There are forty-five of these statements, and each one describes a *subskill*. You answer each statement with a number, using a 5-point rating scale on which 1 means *thoroughly ineffective* and 5 means *highly effective*.

Step 6   Score the assessments, using the method described in Chapter Five.

Note: Although the Supervisor 360° Skill Assessment is designed so it can be self-scored by the supervisor, we recommend that a representative from your organization's Human Resource Department or your direct manager score both the self and observer assessments.

Why Your Self and Observer Scores May Differ

You possess specific skill levels. Ideally, you and your observers will rate your skills at the same levels, and those levels will be equal to your actual skills. In reality, different perspectives and perceptions may prevent you and each of your observers from giving your skills similar ratings. What an inexperienced direct report may see as highly effective skill competency, an experienced frontline worker may see as only adequate. Here are some other reasons for significant variances in observer responses:

- Different observers may have different frequencies of interaction with you, affecting the degree to which they experience your skills.
- Direct reports may see different sides of you than your peers see, and your immediate manager may see yet another side.
- Observers may bring different personalities and expectations to the rating process.
- Observers' own different skill levels may affect their understanding of the rating scale.
- If your roles and responsibilities are not clearly and publicly set, observers may have different ideas of what these roles and responsibilities should be.

Depending on how consistently your observers rate each of your skills and how close your ratings are to the average observer score, you will derive different conclusions and take different actions. If the results are inconsistent, investigate them. Identify the cause of the variance in perceptions in order to separate the skills you need to develop further from the skills you need to publicize more energetically.

Chapter 5

• •

Instructions for Hand-Scoring

The second step in using the Supervisor's 360° Skill Assessment is to understand and analyze your feedback. You can transform your feedback data into highly useful information by filling out the nine spreadsheets in Figures 5.1, 5.2, and 5.3 at the end of this chapter. The completed spreadsheets will identify your overall average self score and overall average observer scores for each of the critical nine supervisory skills. In addition, the spreadsheets will identify your observer score averages for each of the forty-five subskills.

If you have not obtained someone else to score your feedback, you will need to complete this yourself.

To begin self-scoring, turn to the first spreadsheet in Figure 5.1, Communication Skills. Notice that the five subskill statements that relate to this skill area have been identified and briefly paraphrased in the first column of the spreadsheet. These are the five subskills statements from the assessment that measure your overall effectiveness at communication. The number at the beginning of each subskill statement corresponds to its number on the Supervisor's 360° Skill Assessment.

Transfer your responses to these five statements from your self assessment scoresheet to the column titled Self Score on the communication spreadsheet. Next, pick up one of your observer scoresheets. Transfer the answers from that scoresheet into column 1 under the heading Observers' Ratings.

If the observer scoresheet gives N for a score, write N in the appropriate score box. When computing your average scores, subtract the number of N's you receive from the number of observers before dividing that number into the total score. For example, on subskill 14, "Ensuring employees understand job standards," assume that your total observer score is 36. Also assume that ten observers turn in scoresheets but nine give you a number score on this subskill and one gives you an N.

• •

Your average score for this subskill would be 36 divided by 9 (which is 4.00), not 36 divided by 10 (which is 3.60). Failing to include the number of N's in your calculations will dramatically reduce the quality of your feedback data (and show lower scores than you have actually earned).

Continue transferring all your feedback data into the appropriate columns and boxes. When you are through, begin calculating your overall average self score. Add up your five responses and write the resulting total in the total score box in the self score column. Divide that number by 5 (you should have rated yourself on all 45 questions), and write the answer in the overall self average blank.

Now calculate your overall observer average score. Add up all the observer scores in column 1, and write the total in the total score box for that column. Repeat this process for each remaining observer column. Then add up all the individual observer's total scores and write the result in the observer total blank. Next, count the number of observer responses (the number of observers multiplied by the number of subskills) (remember to subtract the number of N's), and write that number in the total number of observations blank. Divide the observer total by the total number of observations and write that result into the observer overall average blank.

The final step is to add up all the observer scores for the first subskill on the spreadsheet and write the total in the subskill total box for that row. Count the number of scores recorded for that subskill (once again ignoring N's), and divide the subskill total by the count. Write the resulting number in the subskill average box. Repeat the process for each of the remaining four subskills on the spreadsheet. You have now completed the spreadsheet for communication skills.

A sample communication skills spreadsheet for a fictitious supervisor is shown in Figure 5.4. The spreadsheet indicates that the ten observers' scores averaged 3.46 for the supervisor's overall communication skills, and that there was some variation in scores across the individual skills.

COMMUNICATION SKILLS

	Self Score	Observers' Ratings												Subskill Total	Subskill Average
		1	2	3	4	5	6	7	8	9	10	11	12		
14. Ensuring employees understand job standards															
18. Giving professional presentations															
25. Listening to others															
32. Resolving interpersonal conflict															
37. Understanding diverse personalities															
Total Score															

Observer Total _____

Total Number of Observations _____

Overall Self Average _____   Overall Observer Average _____

TEAM SKILLS

	Self Score	Observers' Ratings												Subskill Total	Subskill Average
		1	2	3	4	5	6	7	8	9	10	11	12		
3. Building teamwork															
11. Educating on team roles and responsibilities															
22. Keeping the team informed of performance results															
24. Leading productive meetings															
40. Recognizing team success															
Total Score															

Observer Total _____

Total Number of Observations _____

Overall Self Average _____   Overall Observer Average _____

COACHING SKILLS

	Self Score	Observers' Ratings												Subskill Total	Subskill Average
		1	2	3	4	5	6	7	8	9	10	11	12		
5. Counseling employees															
12. Encouraging employees to perform well															
19. Helping employees plan professional development															
29. Positioning employees and using their skills															
31. Providing clear direction and instruction															
Total Score															

Observer Total _____

Total Number of Observations _____

Overall Self Average _____   Overall Observer Average _____

Figure 5.1. **People Skills Spreadsheets**

BUSINESS ANALYSIS SKILLS

	Self Score	Observers' Ratings												Subskill Total	Subskill Average
		1	2	3	4	5	6	7	8	9	10	11	12		
10. Educating staff on their work processes															
16. Estimating the costs of work-related activities															
20. Identifying critical performance indicators															
30. Posting critical performance indicators															
39. Using company data for effective decision making															
Total Score															

Observer Total _____

Total Number of Observations _____

Overall Self Average _____   Overall Observer Average _____

CONTINUOUS IMPROVEMENT SKILLS

	Self Score	Observers' Ratings												Subskill Total	Subskill Average
		1	2	3	4	5	6	7	8	9	10	11	12		
2. Analyzing problems and identifying root causes															
4. Collecting and documenting process information															
13. Ensuring solutions are successfully implemented															
27. Monitoring effectiveness of process improvements															
34. Searching for improvement opportunities															
Total Score															

Observer Total _____

Total Number of Observations _____

Overall Self Average _____   Overall Observer Average _____

COMPUTER SKILLS

	Self Score	Observers' Ratings												Subskill Total	Subskill Average
		1	2	3	4	5	6	7	8	9	10	11	12		
36. Teaching others to use computers and software															
38. Using the computer to write correspondence															
41. Using the computer to analyze performance data															
42. Using the computer to document work processes															
43. Using the computer to search for information															
Total Score															

Observer Total _____

Total Number of Observations _____

Overall Self Average _____   Overall Observer Average _____

Figure 5.2. Technical Skills Spreadsheets

PROJECT MANAGEMENT SKILLS

	Self Score	Observers' Ratings												Subskill Total	Subskill Average
		1	2	3	4	5	6	7	8	9	10	11	12		
1. Accurately estimating project length and cost															
7. Creating detailed action plans															
15. Ensuring specific, measurable, and realistic goals are developed															
21. Keeping other departments informed															
26. Monitoring project progress															
Total Score															

Observer Total _____

Total Number of Observations _____

Overall Self Average _____   Overall Observer Average _____

WRITING SKILLS

	Self Score	Observers' Ratings												Subskill Total	Subskill Average
		1	2	3	4	5	6	7	8	9	10	11	12		
8. Documenting decisions and corrective actions															
9. Documenting standard operating procedures															
17. Filling out company forms															
44. Writing clear and concise reports and memos															
45. Writing with professional grammar and style															
Total Score															

Observer Total _____

Total Number of Observations _____

Overall Self Average _____   Overall Observer Average _____

RESOURCE MANAGEMENT SKILLS

	Self Score	Observers' Ratings												Subskill Total	Subskill Average
		1	2	3	4	5	6	7	8	9	10	11	12		
6. Creating a department budget															
23. Knowing how to obtain scarce resources															
28. Networking effectively															
33. Responding quickly to staff's resource needs															
35. Staying within budget constraints															
Total Score															

Observer Total _____

Total Number of Observations _____

Overall Self Average _____   Overall Observer Average _____

Figure 5.3. Administrative Skills Spreadsheets

COMMUNICATION SKILLS

	Self Score	Observers' Ratings												Subskill Total	Subskill Average
		1	2	3	4	5	6	7	8	9	10	11	12		
14. Ensuring employees understand job standards	2	4	2	4	3	5	3	4	5	4	3			37	3.70
18. Giving professional presentations	2	3	3	3	3	3	3	3	3	3	3			30	3.00
25. Listening to others	3	4	2	4	4	5	4	4	5	4	4			40	4.00
32. Resolving interpersonal conflict	4	3	1	2	3	3	2	3	3	1	3			24	2.40
37. Understanding diverse personalities	4	5	3	2	5	4	5	5	5	3	5			42	4.20
Total Score	15	19	11	15	18	20	17	19	21	15	18				

Observer Total   173

Total Number of Observations   50

Overall Self Average   3.00   Overall Observer Average   3.46

Figure 5.4. Completed Communication Skills Spreadsheet

Chapter 6

• •

Identifying Your Skill Strengths and Needs

Now that you have learned how to calculate your feedback scores, you are ready to turn the data into information useful for your professional development. Use the data from your spreadsheets (or feedback sheets) to answer the following questions. Your first objective is to identify your people, technical, and administrative strengths and weaknesses. After honing in on the larger issues, use the detailed question feedback to uncover the root causes of your successes and missed opportunities. The following exercises and questions will guide you. Please write your answers in the spaces provided.

1. Look at your average scores on the nine people, technical, and administrative skills, and write the skills in order of scoring here, starting with the highest.

   The first skill:

   The second skill:

   The third skill:

   The fourth skill:

The fifth skill:

The sixth skill:

The seventh skill:

The eighth skill:

The ninth skill:

What do you feel are your greatest skill strengths?

What do you feel are your greatest opportunities for skill improvement?

2. Look at your observers' average scores on the nine people, technical, and administrative skills, and write the skills here, in order of scoring from highest to lowest.

The first skill:

The second skill:

The third skill:

The fourth skill:

The fifth skill:

The sixth skill:

The seventh skill:

The eighth skill:

The ninth skill:

What do your observers feel are your greatest skill strengths?

What do your observers feel are your greatest opportunities for skill improvement?

3. Do you and your observers agree on your greatest strengths? How big are the perceived differences? What might explain any differences in perceived strengths?

4. Do you and your observers agree on your greatest opportunities for improvement? How big are the perceived differences? What might explain any differences in perceived improvement opportunities?

5. Overall, are you generally in agreement with your observers, or do your self scores vary greatly from your observer scores?

Analyzing Your Development Opportunities

By now you should be able to identify your lowest-scoring skill of the nine twenty-first-century supervisor skills as perceived by your observers. Your next step is to pull out the spreadsheet for that skill. This page contains your scores on the five subskills that resulted in your overall score for this skill.

For example, let's return to Figure 5.4 and assume this communication skills spreadsheet represents a supervisor's lowest-scoring skill. It presents feedback on five subskills, listed here in order of scoring, from highest to lowest:

1. Understanding, accepting, and adapting to diverse personality and communication styles

2. Listening to others

3. Ensuring every employee understands job standards and expectations

4. Giving professional, informative, and easy to understand presentations

5. Resolving interpersonal conflict

This supervisor scored quite well on three of the five, and poorly on one: resolving interpersonal conflict. Therefore this supervisor can quickly elevate the skill area of communication effectiveness by strengthening his or her conflict resolution skills.

To start your improvement process, look closely at the feedback sheet on your least effective skill. Rank the five subskills in order, starting with the highest observer score.

1. What is your highest-scoring subskill? Was the scoring on it closely grouped (indicating general agreement)?

2. What is your second highest-scoring subskill? Was the scoring on it closely grouped (indicating general agreement)?

3. What is your third highest-scoring subskill? Was the scoring on it closely grouped?

4. What is your fourth highest-scoring subskill? Was the scoring on it closely grouped?

5. What is your fifth highest-scoring subskill? Was the scoring on it closely grouped?

Taking the Next Steps

Now that you have learned how to pick apart your feedback data and prioritize your efforts, identify your ten lowest-scoring *sub*skills out of the forty-five on the assessments and list them in order, starting with the one with the lowest average observer score.

Lowest-scoring subskill:

Second lowest-scoring subskill:

Third lowest-scoring subskill:

Fourth lowest-scoring subskill:

Fifth lowest-scoring subskill:

Sixth lowest-scoring subskill:

Seventh lowest-scoring subskill:

Eighth lowest-scoring subskill:

Ninth lowest-scoring subskill:

Tenth lowest-scoring subskill:

This chapter has given you the opportunity to identify and prioritize your proficiency at the nine skills and their forty-five subskills. If you are working on your own or one-on-one with a manager serving as your coach or mentor, you may want to work on the lower-ranked skills first, strengthening their presence and effectiveness in your daily work. Here are the skills each of the following chapters covers:

- To improve people skills, work with Chapter Seven
- To improve technical skills, work with Chapter Eight
- To improve administrative skills, work with Chapter Nine

If you are going to be part of a class with other supervisors, you may find that working through all the skills in sequence will be easiest. If you are in a classroom environment, take additional time on your own to meet with a manager to discuss those skills you are striving hardest to improve.

It is critical to your leadership that you become competent in all the skills addressed by the Supervisor 360° Skill Assessment. The next three chapters continue the effort to improve your effectiveness. Throughout your learning experience, be quick to ask questions of your facilitator or mentor. Also consider using additional learning resources to further your educational process, including training courses sponsored by your organization. Examine the list of learning resources for each skill found in the Suggested Resources at the end of this workbook.

Good luck—and enjoy your journey of becoming a more effective frontline leader!

Chapter 7

• •

How to Improve Your People Skills

This chapter serves as your personal trainer for the three people skills identified in the Supervisor 360° Skill Assessments: communication skills, team skills, and coaching skills. Collectively, these skills will strengthen your effectiveness as you communicate with others, encourage teamwork, and make presentations.

We provide a number of exercises in order to enhance your learning experience. Write your responses in this workbook, and over the next several months refer back to this workbook as your resource for change.

Exercise   For your first exercise, take a few minutes to review the first three skill areas as they were assessed by your S-360.

1. *Communication skills:* Reflect on the difference between your self score and your average observer score. In your opinion, why is there a difference?

• •

2. *Team skills*: Reflect on the difference between your self score and the average observer score. In your opinion, why is there a difference?

3. *Coaching skills*: Reflect on the difference between your self score and the average observer score. In your opinion, why is there a difference?

Skill #1: Communication Skills

Supervision is a people profession, and communication is the most important professional tool that the twenty-first-century supervisor will possess.
—*Brad Humphrey and Jeffrey Stokes*, The 21st Century Supervisor

Communicating with others can consume 60 to 70 percent of a supervisor's workday. So if the supervisor lacks effective communication skills, the result is likely to be a number of difficulties for employees and ultimately for the company, such as general confusion about job tasks, lack of direction, low morale, and poor performance.

As a leader at the front lines of performance, you must be a proactive communicator. You must be skilled at initiating conversations and discussions about work process problems, facilitating team meetings, presenting and explaining performance reports, and perhaps even conducting customer focus groups.

The three areas of communication skills we address here are (1) listening effectively, (2) understanding and adapting to the communication profiles of others, and (3) facilitating meetings and making effective presentations.

. . . .

Listening: How to Listen More Effectively

Listening permeates everything you do as a supervisor. Listening may be your greatest tool for improving performance—for both you and others. Because listening is so critical to your leadership success and provides the greatest return to you as a supervisor, we will spend considerable time helping you improve this skill. Let's define listening first.

- What do you think is the difference between listening and hearing?

Hearing is the physical capability to perceive noise. For example, you may hear an airplane. There is no message involved, just noise. *Listening* requires a mental process to translate "noise." You listen to others when you hear their words, process the meaning, and understand the message. If you are really listening and do not understand the message, you normally ask questions for clarification.

The Cost of Poor Listening

Listening—real listening—is tough! Most of us hear a lot of stuff during the day, but how many times have you missed something that was said or implied because you were not listening?

Have you ever had an employee come back to you one or more times to ask questions about something you have discussed with him or her? You were sure you had communicated clearly—it was as if the other person had not listened. Unfortunately, this situation is all too common for many supervisors.

A person with poor listening skills might duplicate work efforts or perform assignments that have been changed or rescheduled. Poor listening might lead a person to miss an important scheduled meeting with a customer or patient. A potential for danger arises when people do not listen to a warning presented during a meeting (for example, an instruction to stay away from a particular construction area).

Exercise

Results of Poor Listening

   1. What are some of the negative results experienced in your workplace because someone did not listen? (Do not name the people involved, just briefly identify the negative results.)

   2. Now imagine that everyone in your organization makes one mistake per week due to poor listening. Also imagine that you estimate the cost for each mistake to be $50. (Fifty dollars is a random figure used for this exercise. It is in no way indicative of the average cost associated with poor listening.) Using the following formula, calculate the cost of poor listening to your organization if this error rate were to continue for an entire year.

Number of employees $\times$ $50 $\times$ 52 weeks = $_____

Next make a rough estimate of the costs to your organization of the actual results of poor listening that you listed here. In calculating your per employee figure, include the value of the time wasted because someone did not listen effectively. Such estimates can be difficult to compute (for instance, how much might it cost your company if someone missed an important sales meeting with an interested customer?), but they are eye-opening.

Whether your total cost is huge or small, the figure you arrived at in the exercise still represents a cost due to the lack of a skill that is vitally important to the overall communication process. It is likely that some mistakes due to poor listening cost considerably more than $50 each time they happen. Keep one thing clear in your mind—poor listening costs!

Listening with a Purpose

The act of listening, completed for each word within fractions of a millisecond, is improved by listening with a *purpose*. For supervisors the purpose of listening should always be to understand what the other person is trying to communicate. Consider the following conversation between a supervisor (Steve) and an employee (Kay):

STEVE: Kay, how are you coming on closing out the insurance claims for the Ficklesworth company?

KAY: I just started on the Ficklesworth claims yesterday because you said last week that I needed to close out the Deal claims.

STEVE: Wait a minute. I distinctly remember telling you to hand off the Deal claims to someone else last week because we needed to close out the Ficklesworth claims by the end of this week. Weren't you listening?

KAY: I heard you say to hand off the Deal claims if I couldn't get them closed out by myself in time to get the Ficklesworth claims completed in time. Besides, I thought we had until the end of the month to get the Ficklesworth claims completed.

STEVE: Look, I don't care what you thought you heard. Get going on the Ficklesworth claims right now, or we'll really be behind the schedule.

KAY: I'm so close to finishing out the Deal claims, shouldn't I go ahead and close out those claims?

STEVE: You should have thought about that before now. Give me the Deal claims, and I'll close them out myself—you get on those Ficklesworth claims immediately, or the two of us are going to have a very serious discussion about your poor listening skills.

Exercise   Think about what was actually going on in this conversation.

1. Record your first impressions of the conversation between Steve and Kay.

2. If Steve had really been listening, what should he have understood from his conversation with Kay?

Consider the following lessons that can be derived from Steve and Kay's conversation:

- Steve may not have been clear when he gave Kay new directions the week before.

- Kay is certainly committed to getting the customer's work completed.

- Steve appears to have lost his composure with Kay when he raised the not-so-subtle question, "Weren't you listening?"

- Neither Steve nor Kay seems to practice effective listening. Both of them should start the good listening habit of asking questions for clarity.

Active Listening: Prioritize the Message

Individuals typically employ several levels of listening. First, you might find that you *ignore* the individual speaking, hoping he or she will read your body language and just leave. Second, you might *pretend* to listen, with little eye contact and a stuttering "uh-huh . . . yeah . . . uh-huh . . . I see!" Third, you might be *selective* in your listening, waiting until one of your hot buttons is pushed before you focus.

But it is the fourth level of listening that must be embraced by supervisors— *active* listening. To be active in listening means that you are empathetic: you listen with the sincere desire to understand the intended message and respond appropriately.

Prepare for your next conversation by considering the following techniques for effective conversations. The first two techniques are physical, while the third is a mental technique that improves the process side of listening.

Active Listening Components

1. Pay attention to the messenger.
   a. Make eye contact with the speaker.
   b. Turn your head and body toward the speaker.
2. Identify what is being said.
   a. Record key words and phrases uttered by the speaker.
   b. Establish the purpose of the message or interaction.
3. Prioritize the message.
   a. In the short term:
      - Is an immediate response needed?
      - Is it preferable to redirect this problem, question, or issue to another source?
      - Is it preferable to receive the message in written form?
   b. In the long term:
      - Is an immediate response needed?
      - Is it preferable to schedule a meeting to converse?
      - Is a written record needed for future reference?
   c. Separate the message from the speaker's tone and attitude.
      - Realize that emotional highs and lows can influence a message.
      - Work to bring calm and objectivity to the exchange.
      - Take notes and determine what follow-up should be done with the other person.

You may still use an "uh-huh" or an "I see" from time to time, because these brief verbal expressions can confirm that you are involved in the conversation. However, using these expressions along with the techniques listed previously will change your hearing into listening.

Active Listening: Translate the Message

First and foremost, your purpose should be to understand what the other person is trying to communicate. If you do not correctly translate the message, you are vulnerable to misunderstanding the messenger. This can lead to a premature dismissal of the message or the messenger, hard feelings, or making the wrong decision based on the wrong understanding. Individuals translate messages based on

1. The words used
   - Be aware that words convey only 5 to 10 percent of the intended meaning.
   - Establish a common vocabulary with the speaker.
2. *Filters* (things that influence a person's understanding of the messages he or she receive from others)
   - Personal filters may include biases, values, age, assumptions, emotional hot buttons, and feelings.
   - Company filters may include expectations, experience, knowledge, current information, and needs.
3. The messenger's tone of voice
   - Tone conveys 30 to 40 percent of the intended meaning.
   - Tone may influence the perceptions formed by the listener.
4. The messenger's body language
   - Body language conveys 50 to 65 percent of the intended meaning.
   - Body language includes hand gestures, facial expressions, eye contact, and body posture.

Exercise As you read the following statements, change your tone of voice, eye contact, and body language one by one to experience the different meanings that you might project even though you are saying the same words each time. Work in front of a mirror, or videotape your effort so you can capture the changes in voice tone, facial expression, and so forth.

- "John, when are you going to finish the Johnson project?"
- "I didn't say you screwed up the job report."

As you repeated these statements, did you emphasize them by, for example, changing your voice tone, raising one eyebrow, or pointing your index finger at the imaginary other person? Write a description of how you might appear to another when you make such adjustments in your voice tone or body language. What message might you be sending apart from your verbal message? If you happened to change the wording from what was written here, did it sound more appropriate?

You can see for yourself that you can influence another individual by changing your voice tone or body gestures more than by the actual words you use. In fact, mere words may not always provide the impact you desire when communicating. If you completed this exercise by yourself, try repeating it with another individual and asking for his or her feedback.

This exercise called for you to speak and adjust your voice tone and body language. In real life, the same efforts are made by the individuals with whom you interact. If what you think another individual is saying does not seem to agree with how they are presenting the information, ask him or her to clarify the message. For example, if someone is asking you to assist them in completing a task but is using an angry tone or pointing a finger at you in an almost threatening manner, you might question the severity of the tone or attitude. This person may only be conveying the seriousness of a task to be completed. Or he or she may be upset about something unrelated to the conversation the two of you are having. The important point is to be aware that how a person asks you to help out with a task might influence your perception of the individual, the task, or the importance of the request and might mislead you. If the person really is upset about something, you need to find out exactly what it is.

As a supervisor, how you talk with your employees is just as critical as the words you use. As you experienced in the exercise you just did, changing your voice tone or volume can give others a perception that may not be what you intended. If you are alerting people to an emergency, they certainly should hear and see a greater level of intensity. Conversely, if you desire to create an open, relaxed environment in which others can freely share brainstormed ideas and not feel threatened, then soften your voice tone and use fewer hand movement to reinforce their perception that it is OK to relax.

Active Listening: Analyze the Message

Analyzing, or evaluating, another person's message shows interest on your part and strengthens your understanding of the message. It is critical to include this listening step in the communication process because it helps you respond appropriately.

Your best effort to analyze a message comes through making brief comments and asking short, clarifying questions that invite the individual to expand upon the message or explain specific points to you. Incorporate the comments and questions listed here into your conversations.

- Would you please repeat what you just stated?
- Tell me more.
- Is this what you are saying? (Then, in your own words, state what you think you heard.)
- I'm not clear about what you mean.
- Why do you think this?
- Help me out on this one point. What are you really saying?
- Expand a little on your last statement.
- How does this affect you [or me]?
- What do you want me to do with this information?
- What is your point?
- How did you come to this conclusion [or decision]?

Depending on the complexity of the message, you may choose to ask more questions to gain a thorough understanding. With some messages, you may need to use only a few of these comments and questions, or even none at all.

Remember—to be a better supervisor and frontline leader of people is to be an active listener. This process step of listening is your opportunity to understand each person's message as it was intended. Employees enjoy working for leaders who listen, and the twenty-first-century supervisor will need to be a tremendous listener.

Exercise   Return to the dialogue between Steve, the supervisor, and Kay, the employee, about changing her task. Work with a partner to role-play the situation, but this time use some of the comments or questions just listed, and see what new dialogue results when you have to respond to these remarks instead of making assumptions.

Active Listening: Tips to Improve Your Listening

Finally, let's look at some techniques you can incorporate into your communication efforts. These tips are a good summary of what this chapter has addressed so far.

Tip 1   You must want to listen.

Tip 2   Take notes as others are speaking with you.

Tip 3   Raise your expectations of yourself—and of others.

Tip 4   Listen with your whole body, not just your ears.

Tip 5   Encourage others when listening by giving them your full attention.

Tip 6   Keep personal hot buttons in check. Do not respond before the speaker has completed his or her statement.

Tip 7   Create a good listening environment by looking at the speaker and asking questions that clarify.

Listening is a sure signal to your employees of how much you care about them. It proves to most people whether you respect them or see them only as an aggravation to be tolerated. Leaders in the twenty-first century will discover that the more time they spend listening to others, the more information they will receive. And becoming more informed will make the supervisor more effective as a leader and more valuable as a human resource.

Communication Profiles: How to Understand Others

Most people tend to communicate in a particular way. For example, some individuals prefer to be direct and get right to the bottom line, whereas others tend to be more detail oriented and cautious. As you begin to understand these preferences, or tendencies, of the people you work with, you will enhance your efforts to understand and to be understood.

We use a communication and behavioral inventory to identify the tendencies many people exhibit as they interact with others. This tool is called the Inter-Spective Communication Profile (Humphrey and Stokes, 1999). You may be familiar with similar tools that identify behavioral tendencies. Such knowledge, correctly understood and used appropriately, will greatly improve your interactions with other people.

Following are general descriptions of characteristics of the four main traits identified by the InterSpective Communication Profile (Dominant, Extrovert, Patient, and Conformist). These characteristics are divided into strengths and weaknesses for each trait.

Dominant

Strengths	Weaknesses
Independent	Proud
Productive	Angry or cruel
Optimistic	Domineering
Decisive	Self-sufficient
Strong-willed	Sarcastic
Practical	Unemotional
Determined	Crafty
Confident	Inconsiderate
Leader	

Extrovert

Strengths	Weaknesses
Enthusiastic	Restless
Compassionate	Undependable
Outgoing	Undisciplined
Personable	Weak-willed

Strengths	*Weaknesses*
Talkative	Egocentric
Friendly	Exaggerator
Carefree	Unstable
Warm	Fearful
	Loud

Patient

Strengths	*Weaknesses*
Efficient	Spectator
Practical	Indecisive
Dependable	Self-protective
Conservative	Fearful
Easygoing	Stingy
Diplomat	Unmotivated
Humorous	Selfish
Calm	

Conformist

Strengths	*Weaknesses*
Gifted	Critical
Idealistic	Moody
Sensitive	Theoretical
Aesthetic	Impractical
Analytical	Self-centered
Self-sacrificing	Revengeful
Perfectionist	Unsociable
Loyal	Negative
	Rigid

Exercise   Who are you? Determine the characteristics with which you find your-self operating during a typical workday. Circle the words from the previous lists that best describe your tendencies, whether they are strengths or weaknesses. You

will likely find that most of the characteristics you selected fall in one trait category. Although no individual is exclusively represented by one trait category, most people find that many of their characteristics come from one category.

Learning More About Your Tendencies

To further understand the basic communication traits, read the following lists, and place a checkmark next to the descriptions that you believe apply to yourself.

People who tend toward displaying the Dominant trait may relate to many of these tendencies:

___ Getting results

___ Causing action

___ Accepting challenges

___ Making decisions

___ Questioning the status quo

___ Taking authority

___ Solving problems

___ Providing leadership

People who tend toward being Extroverts may relate to many of these tendencies:

___ Contacting people

___ Making favorable impressions

___ Verbalizing feelings

___ Creating a motivational environment

___ Generating enthusiasm

___ Entertaining people

___ Desiring to help others

___ Participating in a group

People who tend to be the Patient type may relate to many of these tendencies:

___ Being a good listener

___ Calming excited people

___ Demonstrating patience

___ Showing loyalty

___ Developing specialized skills

___ Concentrating on the task

___ Performing an accepted work pattern

___ Setting priorities

People who tend toward the Conformist type may relate to many of these tendencies:

___ Concentrating on detail

___ Critical thinking

___ Checking for accuracy

___ Criticizing performance

___ Being diplomatic with people

___ Working under controlled circumstances

___ Following directives and standards

___ Complying with accepted authority

It is possible for an individual to relate only to one category and not the other three. For example, a person might tend to approach everything in his or her personal and work life by being direct, to the point, bottom-line oriented, and so forth—essentially practicing many of the characteristics relating to the Dominant trait.

However, even though relating to only one trait category is possible, most people find themselves exhibiting behavior and communication characteristics from more than one category. For example, you may be direct and bottom-line oriented with one individual due to the requirements of a job or situation. However, in another situation you may be more extroverted because you are initiating a brainstorming discussion with employees. Still later, you might need to be detail focused to ensure that the end-of-month calculations are correct before you forward a financial report to your manager.

If you find that you relate only to one of the four traits, this simply implies that you prefer, or tend, to approach situations and people from this particular mode. There is nothing wrong with this approach. However, you might consider how the results you experience in some situations might be improved by adjusting the way you approach those situations. Again, if your preference is to be direct and to get to the point with people, you might find that adjusting your approach to be more methodical and detail focused will improve the way you relate to people who perform detailed or analytical work.

If you find more than one of the four categories to your liking, this should encourage you to be sensitive to situations and people around you, adjusting when needed to improve communications and understanding. By incorporating more than one category of tendencies in your communication style, you will greatly enhance your efforts to relate to other individuals and meet the challenge of complex situations.

The next section explores how to interact with people who may or may not share your preferred trait or traits. For example, if you tend to have mostly Patient characteristics, but you find yourself dealing with someone who has mostly Extrovert characteristics, you may need to adjust the way you interact with this person. Making these adjustments may require changing not *what* you say but *how* you say it.

Communication Style Prescriptions

It is time now to consider how you might interact with someone who exhibits a particular set of characteristics. The techniques presented here represent adjustments you may need to make mentally, emotionally, or physically.

Interacting with Dominants

People who display the Dominant trait tend to be direct and use few words. They are sometimes intimidating to others because they may hold eye contact longer than some people wish and because they tend to be competitive and want to "win" discussions. When interacting with someone who displays the Dominant trait be sure to

- Keep the focus on the topic.
- Prepare before presenting.
- Ask the Dominant what he or she wants or thinks.
- Breathe regularly. (Rapid breathing may imply that you are intimidated.)
- Use "you" and "I." (This reinforces your directness.)
- Follow up in writing.
- Keep details short and applicable.
- Maintain eye contact.
- Offer tangible proof or resources.
- Lean slightly forward when sitting or standing.

Interacting with Extroverts

People who display the Extrovert trait are often sociable and friendly, using their verbal capabilities to include others in projects, discussions, and problem-solving opportunities. They sometimes spend too much time talking, dominate conversations, or lose focus on what is most important. When interacting with someone who displays the Extrovert trait be sure to

- Smile and stay upbeat.
- Allow brainstorming.
- Use the Extrovert's name.
- Take notes for review.
- Maintain eye contact.
- Piggyback on the Extrovert's ideas.
- Offer new ideas.
- Loosen up and enjoy the talk.
- Compliment the Extrovert before criticizing.
- Offer ideas from others.
- Ask for the Extrovert's opinion or ideas.

Interacting with Patients

People who display the Patient trait may be reserved and shy. Don't be fooled into thinking that they are uninterested, lazy, or bored. They may simply be waiting for you to initiate a conversation or to ask for their opinion. Patient trait people can frustrate others by their lack of quick response or their lack of outward signs of enthusiasm or support. When interacting with someone who displays the Patient trait be sure to

- Give advance warning: schedule your meetings.
- Be prepared to carry most of the conversation.
- Don't rush the Patient or push him or her to converse.
- Realize the Patient is slower in decision making than others.
- Explain the benefits, both personal and team.
- Greet the Patient cordially, then focus on topic.
- Develop your background, offer testimonies from others about your past successes.
- Allow the Patient to ask questions.
- Provide time for feedback.
- Allow periods of silence.
- Use eye contact less than 60 percent of the time.

Interacting with Conformists

People who display the Conformist trait are often observed as being organized, punctual, and detail focused. Although they may not think of themselves as perfectionists, others may consider them to be so. Conformists can frustrate others by asking questions that would otherwise go unasked. Conformist do not want to make mistakes and often grow cautious about others who (to their way of thinking) do not show proper concern for the "little" things. When interacting with someone who displays the Conformist trait be sure to

- Offer proof of facts, names, dates, and so on.
- Organize; prepare the Conformist for the agenda.
- Let the Conformist play devil's advocate.
- Ask the Conformist about the resources you will need to bring or understand before meeting with him or her.
- Focus on the objectives that the Conformist perceives as critical (for example, measurements, performance results, decisions).
- Relate the topic to future goals.
- Stay on target.
- Encourage the Conformist to tackle new areas.
- Allow time to plan details.
- Allow the Conformist to focus on processes.
- Stay calm and collected.

Exercise You can construct your own communication profile, a picture of your communication preferences. Read and complete each of the following statements to build your communication profile. Your *primary trait* is the trait area (Dominant, Extrovert, Patient, Conformist) that best describes you.

1. My primary trait is:

2. I communicate best by:

3. I need others to:

4. I most respect others who:

5. I listen best when:

6. I participate best when:

Exercise   After completing the previous exercise, share your communication profile information with others, especially your peers and employees. Hold a team meeting with your employees to allow them to complete their own profiles, and encourage each person to share his or her profile with others.

If you and your employees are to experience more effective communication, it is vital for each one of you to understand the needs, strengths, and weaknesses of the others. The communication profile exercise helps each person to educate others about such items. Encourage those who work with and for you to better understand you and your communication profile, as you will try to understand their profiles. By sharing your profile with your peers and employees, you will encourage them to be more proactive in the way they approach you.

This team-building exercise reinforces your better understanding of people, their similarities and their differences. Better knowledge of your own communicator type also helps you work on emphasizing desirable characteristics and overcoming less desirable ones.

Facilitating Meetings and Making Presentations

The third essential area of communication skills involves conducting effective meetings and presenting well-organized information to a group of employees, peers, or managers.

How to Facilitate Meetings

Possessing strong listening skills will improve your efforts to facilitate meetings. As organizations continue to expect greater teamwork, it is important for supervisors to learn how to lead others to make better decisions, solve more complex problems, and to work more cooperatively with others of all levels. Facilitation is a critical skill for accomplishing this.

Facilitating is what you do when you conduct a meeting. Although facilitating requires effective communication (listening, understanding others before speaking, and so forth), there are several additional tools and techniques that can enhance your efforts.

First, every scheduled meeting you facilitate should have a written outline that informs attendees about the subjects that will be addressed. This outline, which should be distributed in advance, is your meeting *agenda*. It helps others prepare for the meeting and assists you in keeping the meeting on target and on schedule.

Second, once you have established an agenda, it is important to appoint someone to take notes during the meeting. You should ensure that this effort is organized and that it is easy for this *recorder* to take notes. The formats shown in Exhibits 7.1 and 7.2 are helpful when preparing for a meeting.

Meeting Outline

Meeting Logistics

TEAM/DEPARTMENT _____   LOCATION _____

FACILITATOR _____   DATE/TIME _____

Meeting Purpose

_____

_____

_____

Meeting Items	TIME ALLOTTED

Meeting Materials	PERSON RESPONSIBLE

Exhibit 7.1. Meeting Outline

Source: Humphrey and Stokes, *TeamGuides*, p. 5. Copyright © 1997 by Brad Humphrey and Jeff Stokes.

Meeting Review

TEAM/DEPARTMENT _____ SCHEDULED TIME _____

DATE _____ ACTUAL TIME _____

Meeting Participants

Subjects Discussed

Who	What	Due Date

Parking Lot

Exhibit 7.2. Meeting Review

Source: Humphrey and Stokes, *TeamGuides*, p. 7. Copyright © 1997 by Brad Humphrey and Jeff Stokes.

Exercise   Make copies of the meeting outline and meeting review forms. Complete a meeting outline prior to your next meeting, and make it available to each individual who will attend the meeting. Ask someone to take notes and to use the meeting review form during the meeting.

Integrating the two forms just addressed into your meeting process should improve meeting participation and help people gain more from your meetings. Be sensitive to the difference such tools can have on your meeting. After using the meeting outline and meeting review forms at your next meeting, create a record here of any observations you made regarding greater comprehension or involvement by those who attended.

Although there is no single correct way to conduct a meeting, the guidelines provided here will strengthen your facilitation efforts:

Step 1   Begin the meeting on time.

Step 2   Prepare your team for participation. Depending on your team's morale or project status, you may find it necessary to adjust your opening to give your team a mental lift. A two-minute icebreaker or a thirty-second pep talk can prepare team members mentally to participate in the meeting.

Step 3   Review the results and decisions of the last meeting. This brings your team up to speed with specific issues. It is also an appropriate time for members to report information gained outside the team.

Step 4   Present the meeting objectives and agenda. Clearly state the purpose of the meeting. Display this purpose during the entire meeting. Write the meeting objectives and agenda on a flip chart or photocopy and distribute them at the beginning of the meeting. Having the purpose and agenda in front of them will help keep the team focused.

Step 5   Implement the agenda. Begin with item one on the agenda, and proceed through the list. Be sure to note the allotted time for each item. Keep the team on track and on time.

Step 6   Allow time for discussion and decision making. Periodically test the team for consensus. Move the team toward decision whenever possible.

Step 7   Create an action plan for every decision. Once your team has made a decision, ask, What's the next step? Insist that an action plan be determined for every decision made. Make sure team members understand task deadlines.

Step 8   Identify objectives for the next meeting. Ask team members for possible topics, and reach consensus on a prioritized list of these topics.

Step 9   Gain team member commitment. Wrap up each meeting with a quick review of decisions made. Remind each member of his or her responsibilities. Sell the team on the fact that the quality commitment of each team member determines the overall success of the team.

Step 10   Adjourn the meeting on time.

How to Make Presentations: Speaking Like a Professional

Making presentations may be one of the most feared tasks a supervisor is asked to perform. However, presentations are nothing more than the verbal delivery of information that addresses specific needs of the audience. Presentations are better when you plan ahead of time what you are going to say, identify the needs of the audience, and practice your presentation.

Follow these steps to improve your presentation skills:

Step 1   Identify your target audience.

Step 2   Brainstorm for your main ideas and subpoints.

Step 3   Prioritize your main ideas.

Step 4   Define the benefits and costs of your ideas.

Step 5   Create an outline of prioritized ideas.

Step 6   Develop handouts and visual aids.

Step 7   Write out your introduction and conclusion.

The time it takes you to plan for a presentation will vary. If the subject is familiar to you and the audience, your planning and presentation time will be less than if you or your listeners are unfamiliar with the topic. Do not assume your audience's knowledge. When in doubt, ask!

Presentations That Are in Balance

Effective presentations bring words, voice tone, and body language into balance. Consider the following guidelines before making your next presentation.

Words

- Use words that are familiar to your audience.
- Be sure that you know the correct pronunciation of your words, especially any technical terms.
- Refrain from using slang or profanity and from telling disrespectful stories.

Voice Tone

- Raise or lower your volume on words or phrases that you want to emphasize.
- Slow your talking speed when drawing attention to a particular point of interest.
- Speak in your normal tone of voice except when you are emphasizing a particular word or phrase.

Body Language

- Maintain eye contact with your audience, moving your focus from person to person or group to group. (Do not look only at one person.)

- Use hand motions to emphasize important points (but not to the extent that your hand motions detract from your message). Don't point your index finger at people; use your whole hand when making an important point.

- Keep your body facing your audience. Don't speak with your back to the audience or stand (hide) behind flip chart easels, tables, or podiums.

Exercise   Ask someone to watch your next presentation and give you honest feedback on your effort. Use every opportunity to make each presentation a chance to improve your skills. Ask the observer to use the assessment form in Exhibit 7.3 to evaluate your presentation and give you organized feedback on all the important areas.

Having an observer assess you on the items in Exhibit 7.3 will help identify areas of your presentation skills that need improvement. Don't be afraid to have someone critique your presentations on a regular basis. The more you can improve in this particular skill area, the more clearly and consistently you will communicate.

Skills #2 and #3: Team Skills and Coaching Skills

The two skills described in this section, team skills and coaching skills, are very important for supervisors. In many work situations these two skills are so closely tied together in the ways they are used that we considered it best to address them jointly.

When building teamwork among any group of people, it is important for someone (in frontline areas the supervisor) to serve in a leadership role to remind, encourage, motivate, and correct the team. The many roles that supervisors fulfill to build teamwork parallel many of the reasons a coach is needed. Although coaching skills are not new, the need for supervisors to enact the coaching role may be new in many organizations.

As today's organizations create formal employee teams, supervisors will be regarded as the coaches of these teams. For that reason the extent to which supervisors learn what makes coaches successful will have a direct impact on their teams' success.

Leading people to work together as a single unit requires great patience, understanding, and consistency. You must be able to talk with your people in such a way that they feel respected. Good coaches look for ways to build their players' skills as they also constantly encourage them on to greater achievement. Here are some coaching tips that can lay the groundwork for greater team success.

- Meet with employees periodically to discuss their roles, responsibilities, job standards, and expectations.
- Use live learning opportunities to pull your people together to discuss a new technique, the failure to meet a performance standard or goal, and similar issues.
- Conduct five-minute huddles at the beginning or end of a shift to address a learning experience from the workday. Let your people share their feedback with you and the other employees.
- Teach your employees what *critical performance measurements* (CPIs) are, why they are important, and how to read these tracking tools. Then have team members update each other at meetings about CPI data and what they have learned. (Refer to *The 21st Century Supervisor* for more information about critical performance measurements.)
- Tie performance efforts by different individuals to overall department performance.
- Have your more experienced people demonstrate proper techniques whenever possible to the other employees in your area.
- Post significant performance standards and goals in clear view of the department, and refer to them during weekly meetings.
- Discuss production, safety, and quality needs every day with your people.
- Maintain consistent eye contact with people.
- When talking to employees, after each point is made, ask if clarification is needed.
- If helpful, demonstrate actions.
- Share important production measurements, and be sure to explain the impact of results, both successes and mistakes, preferably in terms of dollar cost to the company.

Developing Team Responsibility

It is critical to have people accept responsibility. Such acceptance builds greater process ownership by employees and increases trust and cooperation between

Observer's Assessment of Presentation

Organization

1. Did the presentation have an opening?

2. How effective was the opening?

3. Did presenter provide the audience with an outline of what was going to be presented?

4. How effective was the outline?

5. Did the presenter stick to the outline?

6. Did the presenter tie important points to the outline?

7. Did the presenter support his or her points with additional information?

8. Was the additional information credible? Was it the right information?

9. Did the presenter summarize his or her presentation points before closing?

10. How effective was the summary?

11. Did the presenter effectively close the presentation?

Exhibit 7.3. Observer's Assessment of Presentation

Presentation

12. Was the presenter's message clear?

13. Was the presentation easy to follow?

14. Did the presenter *read* the audience (that is, did the presenter speed up, slow down, get louder, get more quiet, and so on based on the needs of the audience)?

15. Did the presenter make enough eye contact with the audience?

16. Did the presenter pause periodically to allow the audience to grasp the intended message?

17. Was the presenter boring? Offensive? Threatening? Friendly? Informative? Motivating?

18. Did the presenter use a projector, handouts, flip chart, or other visual aids?

19. How effective was the presenter at using these visual aids?

20. Did the presenter speak loudly enough for everyone to hear? (Too loudly?)

21. Did the presenter allow for questions from the audience?

22. How did the presenter handle questions from the audience?

23. Did the presentation include any unplanned interruptions? If so, define the interruption.

24. Describe how the presenter handled the interruption.

Exhibit 7.3. continued.

employees. Coach your employees about taking responsibility and stepping up to the plate when the team need arises. Integrate the following techniques into your coaching:

1. *Alert individuals to a need.* It is important to keep your workers alert to issues affecting their safety, quality, operations, and so forth. This may include ensuring that company policies or programs are regularly updated and clarified, and that workers are kept informed about them.

2. *Educate individuals about the need.* This involves training—whether on the job or in the classroom. The level of training depends greatly on the capacity, maturity, and drive of the people.

3. *Engage employees in the implementation plan.* Allowing your employees to contribute their ideas about the way a responsibility can be maintained helps them take ownership of the responsibility. It also allows you to identify the most interested individuals, those who might serve as coordinators for the specific issue. (A coordinator is an employee within the team who more closely oversees a particular work area or project and keeps other team members informed. A coordinator might also be the contact person for the team for the area or project they oversee.)

4. *Define parameters for expectations.* It is important to establish boundaries that can be monitored. These parameters give employees a space in which they can make personal adjustments in what will and will not be tolerated.

5. *Determine and establish costs.* Nonconformance creates costs. The same is true for responsibilities that are not fulfilled. Coordinators and employees must realize the costs associated with not fulfilling a responsibility.

6. *Provide ongoing support.* Supervisors must make the support effort continuous. Although individual attention is always possible, most of your efforts will be directed through a coordinator.

Driving Teamwork

You must constantly look for daily opportunities where some adjustment on the part of a worker can improve his or her efforts and create more team success; when you can assist in this adjustment you will be driving people toward better teamwork. Don't be surprised by the simplicity of such opportunities.

Based on your department's current work effort, list activities that might easily be improved if teamwork were practiced among two or more employees.

When any of the situations you have just recorded appear, consider using the following coaching techniques to drive teamwork:

Step 1   Ask the employee involved if there is an easier, more effective way to complete the same task.

Step 2   Based on the employee feedback, thank him or her for the idea.

Step 3   If time allows, try the employee idea.

Step 4   As the idea is being exercised, observe and coach the effort.

Step 5   If the effort is successful, encourage the method to be repeated whenever the situation recurs. If the effort is not successful, discuss the reasons for failure with the employee. Discussing the failed idea will encourage the employee to try again and assure him or her that you are not angry over the failure.

Pure Coaching

Three efforts must find their way into your coaching: (1) providing positive reinforcement, (2) challenging employees without provoking, and (3) modeling the right behavior. Perhaps the greatest people skill challenge to these three efforts is a problem employee. For our purposes here, we will define a problem employee as an individual who refuses to follow the processes or procedures of the organization or department. A problem employee may also be an individual who displays behavior that is unprofessional, offensive, or threatening or that undermines the leadership of supervisors or other leaders or the integrity of the organization.

When coaching the problem employee, follow these steps:

Step 1   Schedule a meeting with the individual, and inform him or her of the reason for the meeting.

Step 2   Keep your voice tone low and in control during the entire encounter.

Step 3   When the employee arrives at the meeting, ask if he or she is aware of the problems you want to address.

Step 4   Whether the individual is aware or not, present the problem issues, including clear and accurate proof.

Step 5   Offer the employee time to respond.

Step 6   Present the results that will be expected, and ask the individual if he or she would like to work with you to bring about those results.

Step 7   If the employee is interested in working with you on a solution, proceed. If not, present to him or her the steps that you see need to be taken to correct the problem. Be sure to provide clear direction.

Step 8   Determine an appropriate time period for completing the corrections, with a specific completion date. Schedule meetings throughout that time frame to discuss the individual's progress.

When Coaching Turns to Counseling

Sooner or later, you will have a problem employee who will not respond to positive reinforcement, challenges, or the so-called velvet hammer. (The velvet hammer is a manner of disciplining a problem employee. For example, a leader might say, in a calm, nonthreatening tone of voice, to an employee with an absenteeism problem, "You know, James, if you miss many more days from work, I'm not going to be very happy. You don't want me to be unhappy do you?" In this way the supervisor softens the punch of stating that the developing situation is serious yet lets the employee know that the problem must be dealt with. Take away the velvet from the hammer, and the same supervisor might have said, "James, if you miss two more days, you're fired.")

When this employee moves you to take more dramatic steps, remember that it is still important for you to handle him or her with respect and objectivity. Incorporate the following counseling steps into your coaching:

Step 1   Make sure that your counseling is done in private.

Step 2   If you are counseling a person of the opposite sex, have a third party sit in to witness the counseling effort. (Ask your human resource manager to suggest a witness.)

Step 3   Inform the employee of the reason for the counseling.

Step 4   Invite the employee to express his or her views first; listen actively.

Step 5 Refrain from poking holes in the employee's views. Gently confront the behavior or attitude that is unacceptable and areas where there is disagreement.

Step 6 Inform the employee of the impact the company, the department, and other employees are experiencing as a result of the problem.

Step 7 Provide suggestions for improving or correcting the problem.

Step 8 Offer to work with the employee to develop an action plan for making needed improvement.

Step 9 Schedule a follow-up meeting to discuss improvement efforts and results.

Step 10 Bring your counseling session to a close by informing the employee that the next effort will be more formal. (If the Human Resource Department will be part of the employee's next experience, make sure that the individual understands this.)

Exercise Find some good models for your coaching.

1. Think about the coaches you played for while growing up. (If you did not play sports, reflect on a famous coach of the last ten to twenty years.) What made the most successful ones effective?

2. Think about some of the best supervisors and managers you have worked for in your career. What made them successful? List some of their leadership characteristics that you most admire.

3. Look at your answers to the first question, and compare them with your answers to the second question. What are some of the leadership strengths that your effective previous supervisors or managers had in common with the best coaches?

4. Placing your people in the right jobs is critical to maintaining their personal motivation and achieving successful team results. Consider the people who report to you. Do you feel some of them are in the wrong job or position? Describe why one of these individuals may be in the wrong position, and what you can do to reposition him or her.

5. Is someone who works for you currently becoming a problem? Describe the nature of the problem.

6. Is the person you just identified causing a disturbance for your other employees? If so, you may need to apply some of the guidelines presented in this chapter. Write out a few steps that you might apply with this individual, keeping your focus on his or her improvement.

People Skills in Review

This chapter is the longest of the skill chapters. Perhaps that is because the heart and soul of supervision is people. It is critical to your future success as a supervisor and to the performance improvements of your people that you fully grasp the significance of improving your people skills.

Supervision is not sitting in the bleachers as a spectator. Supervision in the twenty-first century will require your full participation. It will require your commitment to get in the middle of things, to involve yourself with other people, and to make sure that the direction you are setting will benefit your company and those your company serves.

Supervision requires you to be honest, to be objective, and foremost, to possess integrity. Integrity means that you feel compelled to do the right thing, in every situation, no matter who is watching. You must be the leader who your managers, peers, and employees can count on to be there when needed and to create the environment in which others can succeed.

Accomplishing such success will require you to be effective in your people skills. Before venturing on to the technical and administrative skills, look again at the differences between your self scores and observer scores. Consider the efforts you need to make to raise your scores. As you raise your score in the months and years to come, watch your employees' performance improve.

Perhaps the greatest compliment a supervisor can receive is for his or her people to become leaders within the organization. A good sign that you are doing things well is that you lose some of your best employees periodically to promotion and advancement. Good luck as you improve your people skills.

Chapter 8

How to Improve
Your Technical Skills

Most supervisors think of technical skills as hands-on knowledge of equipment and machinery. Although this definition will continue to be important in some areas, additional technical skills are necessary for all twenty-first-century supervisors. A brief review of the technical skills spreadsheets for your Supervisor 360° Skill Assessment will point to the new additions.

The most technical skill assessed is your effectiveness at using the computers in your work area. The two other technical skills involve your effectiveness at analyzing the business side of your department, and your success at driving continuous improvement. Both skills require you to use paper tools for carrying out analysis, measurement, and monitoring.

Exercise   Take a few minutes to review the second three skill areas as they were assessed by your S-360.

1. *Business analysis skills:* Reflect on the difference between your self score and your average observer score. In your opinion, why is there a difference?

2. *Continuous improvement skills*: Reflect on the difference between your self score and the average observer score. In your opinion, why is there a difference?

3. *Computer skills*: Reflect on the difference between your self score and the average observer score. In your opinion, why is there a difference?

Skill #4: Business Analysis Skills

Good supervisors and their employees want to work smarter, not harder. Your organization should provide performance information about how well the organization is doing and/or how well your department is performing.

Exercise　Begin thinking about the performance information that would help you and your team reach your goals.

1. Record two or three formal measurements that your organization provides.

2. Describe how you use this information in being a more effective supervisor.

3. Do your employees understand this information? Why or why not?

Cost of Quality

The first step toward acquiring better business analysis skills is to understand how much poor quality or performance costs your organization. This cost is called the *cost of quality* (COQ).

Example   You supervise twenty employees. If every employee wastes just fifteen minutes each day looking for supplies or resources that were misplaced, you could calculate the cost of quality for this seemingly minor problem as follows:

1. 20 people $\times$ 15 minutes per day $=$ 300 minutes per day, or 5 hours per day
2. 5 hours per day $\times$ 265 work days per year $=$ 1,325 hours per year (annualized projection)
3. 1,325 hours per year $\times$ \$15 per hour average pay rate $=$ \$19,875 per year in lost time and therefore lost performance (annualized projected COQ)

What could your employees accomplish if they had an additional 1,325 hours to work? Although this COQ may not sound high in terms of pure dollars, consider the further cost associated with the work that did not get accomplished during those 1,325 hours of nonperformance.

Exercise   Develop your own cost of quality. Using the previous example as a model, calculate the COQ for an activity or process in your department that is a problem. Use the project cost of quality form in Exhibit 8.1 to assist in your calculations.

Work Flow

You must understand the work processes in your department and know more about work processes in your organization. These processes (called *work flows*) drive the business of your organization. Study the example of a customer order work flow in Exhibit 8.2.

To give a clear picture of work flow, a *flowchart* is normally used. When you use a flowchart you can more clearly recognize the critical performance indicators (CPIs) that reflect how well a particular work process is performing. Exhibit 8.3 is a flowchart of the customer order work flow shown in Exhibit 8.2.

Project Cost of Quality

NAME _____ DATE _____

Project Description _____

_____

_____

Labor Expense _____

COST/HOUR	X	# OF PEOPLE	X	# HOURS/DAY	=	TOTAL COST/DAY	ANNUALIZED
$ _____		_____		_____		$ _____	$ _____

INCLUDES

_____

_____

Equipment Expense _____

COST/HOUR	X	# OF PEOPLE	X	# HOURS/DAY	=	TOTAL COST/DAY	ANNUALIZED
$ _____		_____		_____		$ _____	$ _____

INCLUDES

_____

_____

Material Expense _____

COST/UNIT	X	# UNITS/DAY	=	TOTAL COST/DAY	ANNUALIZED
$ _____		_____		$ _____	$ _____

INCLUDES

_____

_____

Total Cost of Quality Expense for 1 Year $ _____

Comments _____

_____

_____

Exhibit 8.1. Project Cost of Quality

Source: Humphrey and Stokes, *TeamGuides*, p. 57. Copyright © 1997 by Brad Humphrey and Jeff Stokes.

Exercise Using the COQ example you described earlier, write down the steps that should be followed when performing that particular task. Be sure to record them in the order in which they should be performed and then number them.

After numbering the steps, show the list to your employees to ensure you have not missed any steps. Then ask them to analyze each step to see where a mistake might possibly be made. Identify the most critical items to be finished or satisfied for the process to be completed without mishap. These items are your critical performance indicators. CPIs are key because they represent the most important measurements your employees must follow. When the data for a CPI fall below expectations or requirements, you and your employees should initiate a problem-solving effort to correct the situation.

Identifying and monitoring several CPIs in your work area also unites your employees as they begin to realize that what they do contributes to the CPI measurement. This is a terrific way to drive more teamwork from within your workforce.

Next, as employees begin to share an interest in achieving better results and as those critical performance indicators are identified, your employees will want to see their daily, weekly, or monthly *scores*, the results of tracking those indicators. We call the presentation of such measurements the team scorecard, and it is the topic of the next section.

1. Customer order is received.

2. Order is processed in data entry.

3. Order is placed in production schedule.

4. Order is sent to production floor.

5. Order is produced.

6. Completed product is sent to holding area.

7. Accounting forwards billing information to warehouse.

8. Shipping receives release documentation for order.

9. Shipping manifest is created.

10. Does billing material match order? If yes, go to Step 11. If no, go to Step 10a.

    10a. Contact Accounting Department.

    10b. Is billing invoice correct? If yes, go to Step 5. If no, go to Step 10c.

    10c. Obtain correct invoice. Go to Step 11.

11. Order is loaded onto truck.

12. Copies of shipping documentation are returned to Accounting and Customer Service.

13. Accounting transfers order to accounts receivable.

14. Customer Service communicates shipping date to customer.

15. Customer's account is credited when payment is received.

Exhibit 8.2. Customer Order Work Flow

Building a Team Scorecard

It is important to keep your employees informed on current performance results. The information should reflect the very heartbeat of the department. For example, if the results reflect negative performance, the employees will realize that inspection, analysis, and improvement are required.

Exercise In the left-hand column on page 81, identify three to five performance items that are critical to your department's success. In the right-hand column, note how each one is measured. (For example, customer complaints might be measured by frequency of occurrence, or scrap and waste might be measured by weight or quantity.)

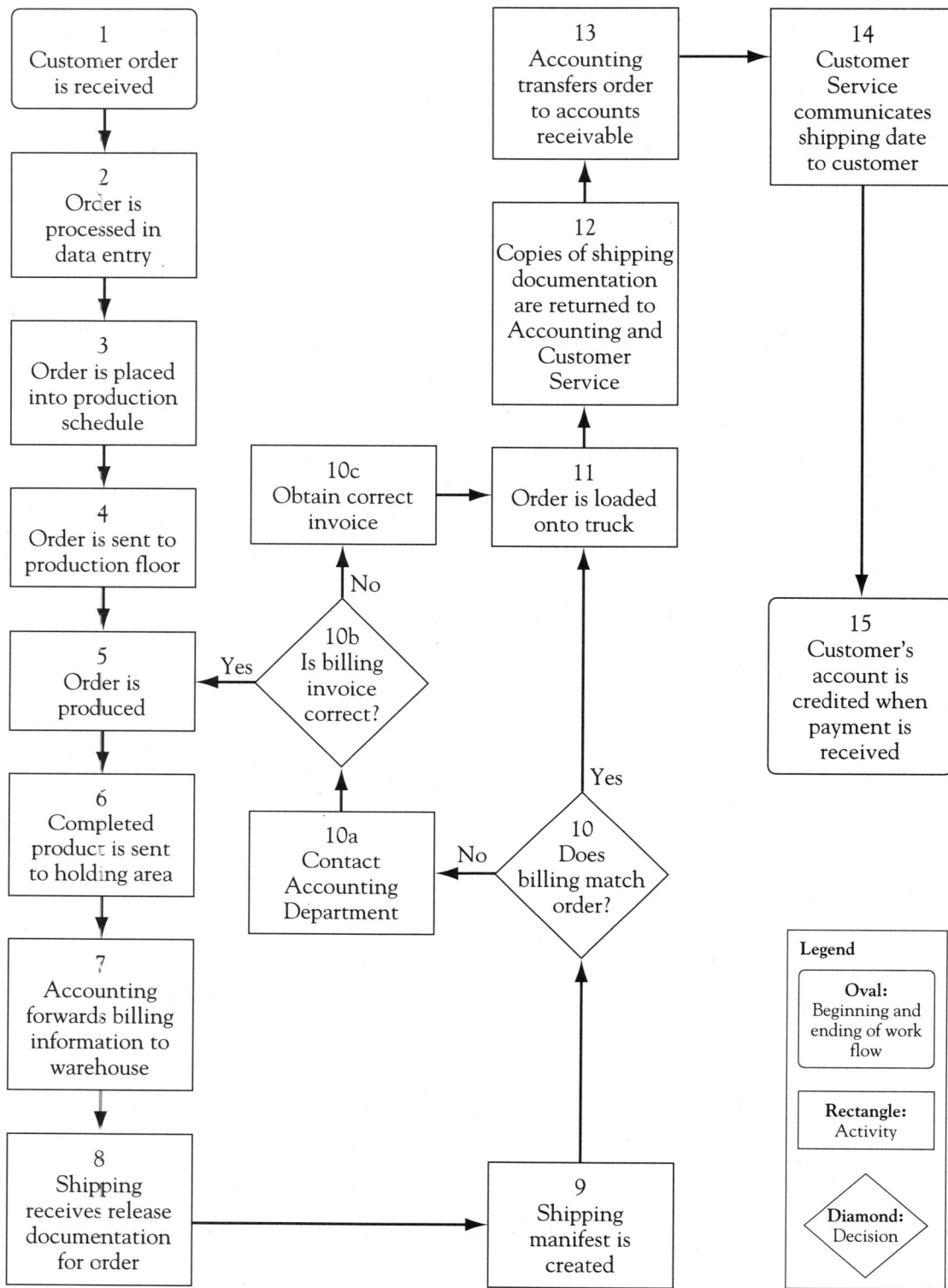

Flowchart Boxes

1 Customer order is received

2 Order is processed in data entry

3 Order is placed into production schedule

4 Order is sent to production floor

5 Order is produced

6 Completed product is sent to holding area

7 Accounting forwards billing information to warehouse

8 Shipping receives release documentation for order

9 Shipping manifest is created

10 Does billing match order?

10a Contact Accounting Department

10b Is billing invoice correct?

10c Obtain correct invoice

11 Order is loaded onto truck

12 Copies of shipping documentation are returned to Accounting and Customer Service

13 Accounting transfers order to accounts receivable

14 Customer Service communicates shipping date to customer

15 Customer's account is credited when payment is received

Legend

Oval: Beginning and ending of work flow

Rectangle: Activity

Diamond: Decision

Exhibit 8.3. Customer Order Flowchart

Performance Item   *How Measured*

A team scorecard is nothing more than a means of posting the most critical measurements—and then keeping such information up to date. Figure 8.1 depicts a sample scorecard for production.

Exercise   Build your own team scorecard for your department that tracks your CPIs. If you have access to a computer, use it to print graphs or charts that help people visualize what performance numbers mean.

Skill #5: Continuous Improvement Skills

The term *continuous improvement* implies that things can always be improved; what is done tomorrow can be better than it was yesterday. Although continuous improvement does not suggest constant change for change's sake, it does require supervisors to always be on the lookout for processes and procedures that can be improved.

Some improvement opportunities are obvious; some are not so easy to see.

Scrap

Rework

Preventive Maintenance Completed

Hours Worked Per Unit

On-Time Production

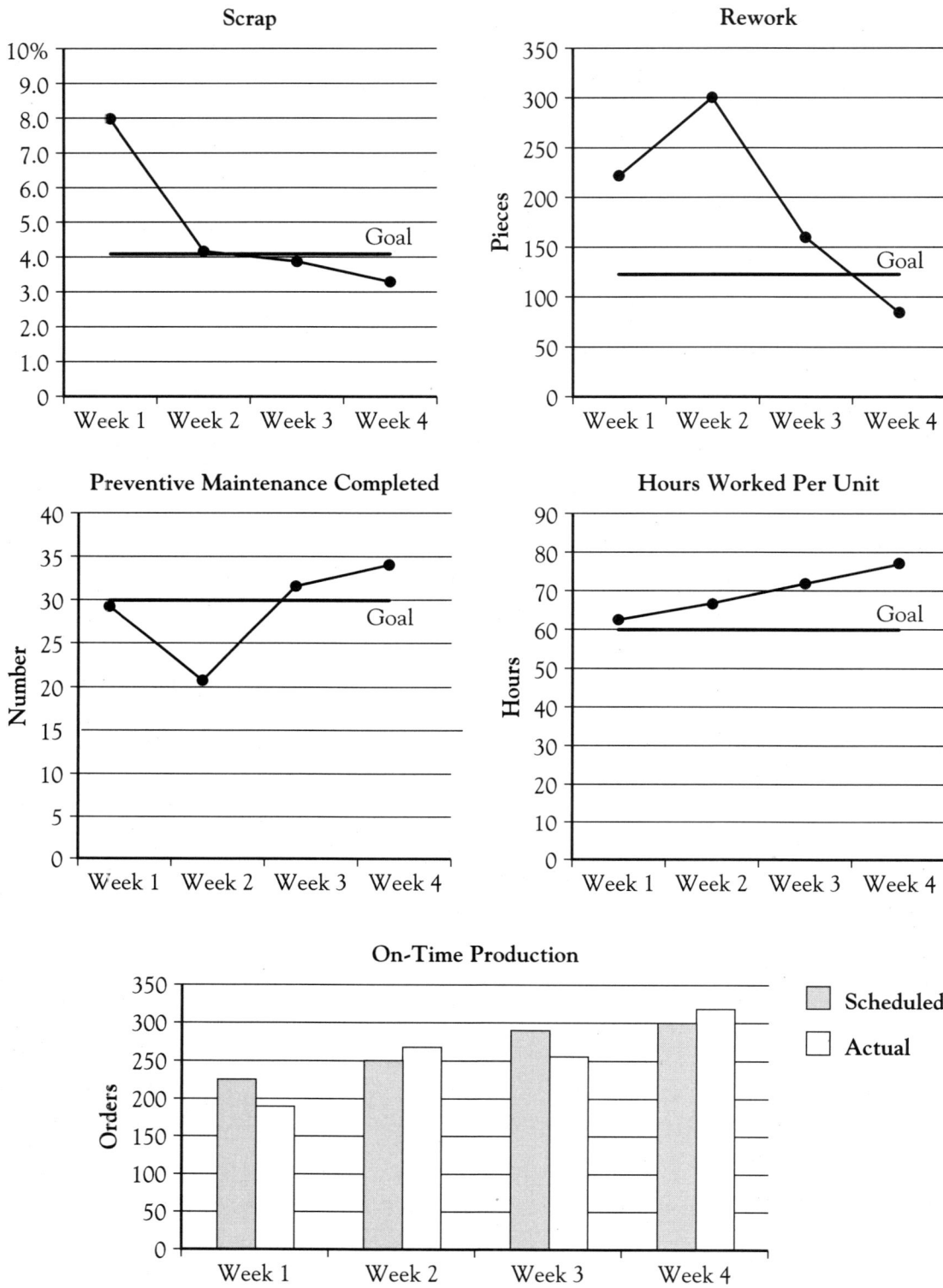

Figure 8.1. Four-Week Production Team Scorecard

- List some work-related items in your department that need improvement:

Not every improvement opportunity needs a team effort or a long, heavily documented, problem-solving process to present to upper management. Some improvements are as simple as one person making a minor change in the way he or she performs a task. However, when process problems become bigger than one person can handle, a formal problem-solving process may benefit overall continuous improvement.

Problem-Solving Model and Process

In order to positively affect continuous improvement, you must learn how to problem solve and how to use available resources and tools that can ensure you arrive at the best possible solution.

We have developed the following Problem-Solving Model, which is simple to use and to teach to your employees. Let's look at the model first (Figure 8.2) and then begin to work through a problem your department is experiencing.

Exercise   Select an activity or process in your department that is a problem, and apply the Problem-Solving Model. You may want to involve your employees in this process. Feel free to refer back and forth to this section and the steps described here as you solve the problem that is your opportunity for improvement. You may also want to refer to the business analysis skills described earlier for more information on developing a cost of quality projection.

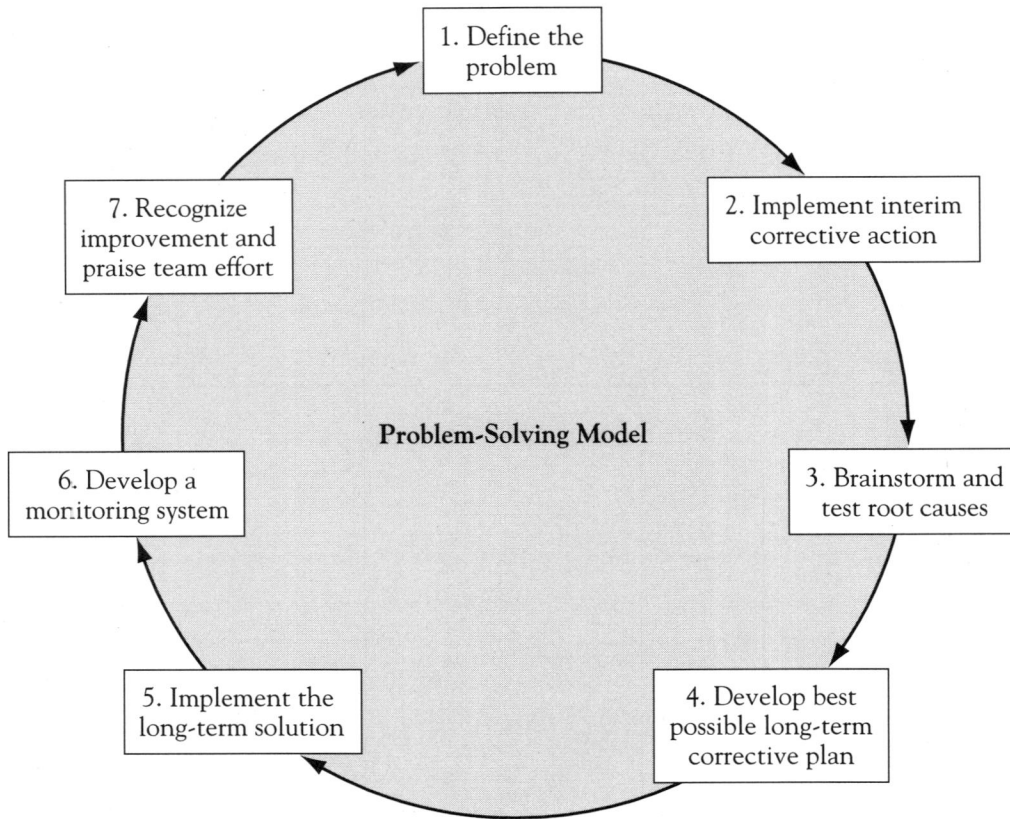

Problem-Solving Model

1. Define the problem

2. Implement interim corrective action

3. Brainstorm and test root causes

4. Develop best possible long-term corrective plan

5. Implement the long-term solution

6. Develop a monitoring system

7. Recognize improvement and praise team effort

Figure 8.2. Problem-Solving Model

Step 1   Define the problem. Write a problem statement that clearly and accurately describes the problem at this time. (Be careful that you do *not* state why you think the problem is happening, because this assumption about the cause may persuade you to the wrong solution.)

Step 2   Implement interim corrective action. Have you put any form of short-term, interim, corrective action into place to shore up possible problems? (This step is nicknamed the Band-Aid step, because this short-term solution may not be the same as the long-term solution.) Describe any interim corrective action that you have tried or that could be explored while you search for a long-term solution. (You may want to brainstorm this Band-Aid effort with your employees.)

Step 3   Brainstorm and test root causes. In this third step, you facilitate others to brainstorm possible causes of the defined problem. Schedule a meeting with your employees, and lead them through a seven- to ten-minute brainstorming effort. You may want to use a brainstorming tool similar to the one shown in Exhibit 8.4. Keep a list of the brainstormed ideas, and then test the most credible causes. Testing may require you and your employees to record frequency or length of problem occurrence, cost of the occurrence, impact of the occurrence on performance, and so on.

Step 4   Develop the best possible long-term solution. This fourth step should be exercised only when you are confident that you have determined the most likely root cause for the problem. Once you have made this determination, then develop a solution that corrects the problem for the long term. Put your solution in writing, and obtain your manager's agreement to it. Inform every individual who is involved in any way with the work process. It is also wise to create an action plan, similar to the one shown in Exhibit 8.5., for implementing the solution.

Step 5   Implement the long-term solution. The fifth step is nothing more than alerting other individuals about the implementation plans—and then putting the proposed solution into action. The key to this step's success is to secure all the needed resources and notify every individual who might be affected by the change. Any education or training that is required should be completed prior to implementing the solution.

Brainstorming

Situation _____

_____
_____
_____

Brainstormed Ideas	SUGGESTED BY	PRIORITY (A, B, C)

Brainstorming Guidelines

1. Select a facilitator.
2. Establish a time limit (4-7 minutes).
3. Stimulate team participation (no critical feedback).
4. Prioritize ideas (A, B, C).

Exhibit 8.4. Brainstorming

· ·

Source: Humphrey and Stokes, *TeamGuides*, p. 21. Copyright © 1997 by Brad Humphrey and Jeff Stokes.

Action Plan

DEPARTMENT _____ SPONSOR _____

Goal _____

_____

_____

_____

_____

ACTION STEPS	PEOPLE RESPONSIBLE	COMPLETION DATE	RESOURCES NEEDED

Exhibit 8.5. Action Plan

Source: Humphrey and Stokes, *TeamGuides*, p. 39. Copyright © 1997 by Brad Humphrey and Jeff Stokes.

Step 6   Develop a monitoring system. Avoid the mistake many supervisors have made when implementing a solution—assuming that everything related to the solution will work fine. Often a problem that has been solved will reappear unless a monitoring system is in place to ensure that the solution continues to be implemented correctly and continues to be improved. So identify the best way to monitor the solution. You might select individuals who will gather data that indicates how the solution is performing. It is also important to formally discuss the new results on a weekly or monthly basis to ensure that everyone involved with the solution is satisfied with the results. A new flowchart for work process with the solution in place will help educate everyone about the solution and serve as a monitoring tool.

Step 7   Recognize improvement and praise team effort. If the solution is successful, plan to recognize those individuals who were part of the problem-solving process. You can do this by describing their efforts in the company newsletter, writing a positive letter of achievement for their employee file, buying the team dinner or lunch, and the like.

Driving Continuous Improvement

Driving continuous improvement requires you to keep the challenge of improvement constantly before your people. Your passion to see problems solved will ignite greater enthusiasm for problem solving among your employees and raise their expectations about pursuing the best possible performance.

Here are some additional efforts (to-do's) you can make to drive continuous improvement in your department:

- Develop and maintain your department's own team scorecard.
- Post the performance results, in graph or chart form, that are most critical to your department's success.
- Conduct a quarterly audit on the performance of your department.
- Involve your employees in this audit, and let them assess for themselves the current condition of the department and its various components. Create a simple rating system to measure these components (such as a 1 to 3 rating system, in which 1 means *below expectations*, 2 means *meets expectations*, and 3 means *exceeds expectations*).
- Survey your internal customers and suppliers (those inside your company) twice a year so you and your employees can hear how effectively your department is performing in terms of meeting their needs.

A short survey, with perhaps five questions that allow others to comment on important department functions, is all it takes to receive helpful feedback.

- Get in the habit of asking your employees this question: "What can we do better?"

- Don't overlook the obvious. Periodically, ask your employees about the status quo and whether or not any improvement can be reached. Look for simple opportunities (such as resolving a situation in which the same mistake is being made again, and again, and again).

Skill #6: Computer Skills

Besides public speaking and making presentations, using a computer has become the next biggest nightmare for many supervisors. But just as it is possible to overcome the fear of public speaking and to become a competent presenter once you know some basic steps and guidelines, it is not especially difficult to learn to operate a computer with proficiency once you plunge in and start learning. And regardless of how you feel about computers, you must integrate their use into your supervisory efforts.

The computer can be your best technical friend because it can help you:

- Monitor production, quality, and safety needs (it can be tied directly into your production equipment)

- Project outlines, statistics, key points, and graphs onto screens during presentations

- Contact sources of information outside the organization through the Internet

- Coordinate production with the purchase of supplies (often called material requirement planning, or MRP)

- Develop communication or personality profiles to enhance your understanding of your employees

- Conduct new employee orientation

- Monitor customer complaints

- Design blueprints for products, parts, and buildings

- Develop and track reports, letters, and forms

Computer Software Programs

The following information defines many of the programs available to you. At the conclusion of each definition, list the names of the software programs that your organization provides for your use.

Word Processing Software

The primary purpose of word processing programs is to simplify and enhance the writing of letters, memos, reports, meeting notes, and the like. Word processing software continues to improve, with more document formats and graphics such as charts becoming available in each software upgrade.

- My organization uses the following software program(s) to accomplish word processing:

Spreadsheet Software

Now you will find out how easy it was for your manager to create those complicated charts and graphs. Spreadsheets are most often used to analyze financial information, to analyze performance or productivity results and trends, and to perform quality analysis.

- My organization uses the following software program(s) to create and manage spreadsheets:

Presentation Software

Whatever used to be done with slides, transparencies (overheads), and videos can now be accomplished with the computer. Presentation software will give most any presentation you make a more professional image. You will also spend less time changing transparencies or making sure your slides are not turned upside down in the projector. Create your presentation material on your computer, network the computer to a projector, and you are in business.

- My organization uses the following software program(s) to assist with presentations:

Database Software

Database software is the best organizer of information that exists. You might, for example, use a database to maintain and organize your contacts' names, addresses, telephone numbers, fax numbers, e-mail addresses, and so on. You can also keep significant information about your contacts to remind you of special occasions or needs. You can also create one copy of a letter or report and have the database automatically address that document to many different people at different addresses. Other database applications might focus on managing the organization's financial information, tallying survey results, or monitoring performance of equipment or machinery—to name only a few.

- My organization uses the following software program(s) to create and maintain databases:

E-Mail Software

E-mail is one of the most exciting thing happening with computers today—and the future looks even more exciting. With a hookup to a telephone line, you can communicate with anyone in the world who has an e-mail address. If your job requires a lot of interaction with others (especially persons not in your immediate area), e-mail provides you with another way of communicating with them and of sending them documents such as reports, memos, or letters over the phone line.

- My organization uses the following software program(s) for e-mail:

Browser Software

Browsers allow you to surf the Net, that is, visit Internet sites. Still young compared to other computer applications, the Internet will be a major resource for you as a leader. Thousands of organizations have established a presence on the Internet by developing Web sites. As organizations learn to use the Internet more for commercial purposes than simply for posting information, extraordinary interactivity among customers and suppliers will result. It will become easier for you to do business with many of your suppliers because of the Internet. Be patient, it will happen!

- My organization uses the following software program(s) as Internet browsers:

Flowcharting Software

We have already addressed the need for supervisors to understand work flow and to be able to diagram how work in their area is completed. Flowcharting applications enable you to create charts that clearly identify the work being done at each step of a process, how it is done, and who is involved with it. Commonly accepted symbols are used to indicate types of work activity, when a decision is to be made, and so on.

- My organization uses the following software program(s) for designing flowcharts:

This list has described many computer applications. There are others—and still more to come every year. However, at this time let's assess where you believe your skills are as they relate to computers.

Exercise In the left-hand column of the following space, compile a list of the software applications available to you through your organization. (Refer to your responses from the last few pages.) In the center column, assess your effectiveness with each application. Be honest about your level of proficiency. Then, in the right-hand column, make a note of how you might achieve the needed improvement (for example, use the software more often, take a class on the software application, secure a book about the software).

Software
Applications   *Proficiency*   *Ways to Improve*

Coaching Your Teams on Computers

The intensity of your efforts to educate and coach your team members about computers will vary depending on each individual's current understanding. However, regardless of employees' current level of understanding and experience, a great part of your coaching effort in the future will be to bring greater computer availability and resources to employees.

For Teams with Little Computer Experience

- Introduce employees to the benefits of computers through articles and videotapes.

- Invite people from other teams or companies that have had positive experiences with computers to visit your team and share their stories.

- Schedule a tour of other departments or companies that are successfully using computers so that your employees can get a better grasp of how computers can be integrated into a department.

- Conduct a brainstorming session with your team members to identify current work areas that could be improved if more information were available. Then show them how computers can supply the needed information.

- Bring a computer into the work area, and allow employees to play a simple computer game or do an easy exercise so that they can experience computers in a nonintimidating way.

For Teams with Computer Experience

If your team members are proficient with computers, allow them the freedom to seek out additional software applications that will enhance their performance and effectiveness. Encourage individuals on your team to cross-train on software applications in which they are not as proficient. Motivate those employees who are proficient in a particular software program to educate those who are not. Sharing this knowledge will build a more educated team of people, and one that really enjoys working together and that appreciates the benefits each person provides to the overall team effort.

Technical Skills in Review

The technical skills assessed by the S-360 reflect your effectiveness as a leader, decision maker, and problem solver. Your organization needs you to become more effective and efficient in your efforts to raise performance.

In the past, supervisors were often told when performance was poor or when something in their department needed to be improved. The twenty-first-century supervisor is expected to identify improvement needs when they appear, conduct a thorough investigation of the problem, facilitate the analysis process by employees to produce a solution, and finally, implement the new solution. The sooner you are capable of providing this kind of leadership, the sooner you will see performance improvement in your department and more profitable recognition for yourself.

The computer will play a central role in your efforts to lead, decide, and solve problems. As you will discover in the next chapter, the computer will also assist you in locating resources. If you are still not confident about your computer skills, start today to look for assistance, both inside and outside the company. Take a class on your own if necessary. The future benefits will be well worth the price.

If you are already comfortable operating a computer, look for more software applications that your department can use. Involve more of your employees in operating computers. One positive mark supervisors can make on a company is to raise other employees' aptitude in technical skills. Begin making your mark by coaching your employees for greater technical knowledge in business analysis skills, continuous improvement skills, and computer skills.

Chapter 9

How to Improve
Your Administrative Skills

Administrative skills address mostly the management side of leadership. Even more than people and technical skills, administrative skills require planning, foresight, and a higher level of involvement by the supervisor.

Possessing effective administrative skills will separate you from other supervisors. Improving your abilities in the first two skill areas (people and technical) help you develop your employees into better performers and improve department performance and ultimately organization performance. Improving your administrative skills will have a direct and immediate impact upon the performance of your organization.

Developing your administrative skills will empower you to take charge of planning projects and work schedules, keeping your senior managers and customers up to date and securing every possible resource for greater performance results!

Exercise   Take a few minutes to review the three administrative skill areas as they were assessed by your S-360.

1. *Project management skills:* Reflect on the difference between your self score and your average observer score. In your opinion, why is there a difference?

2. *Writing skills:* Reflect on the difference between your self score and the average observer score. In your opinion, why is there a difference?

3. *Resource management skills:* Reflect on the difference between your self score and the average observer score. In your opinion, why is there a difference?

Skill #7: Project Management Skills

Successful project management begins at the end. You cannot achieve that end (a completed project or task) without having a vision of where you want to go.

Exercise   Just as your organization has a vision, so should you have a vision for your department.

1. What do you think is your organization's vision for the future?

2. As you consider your firm's vision of the future, also consider the future of your own department, and complete this statement:

One year from today I would like to see my department experience the following successes:

3. Now, write a vision statement for your department in one or two sentences. Make sure it is easy to understand. (Here is a sample vision statement: "My vision for my department is to see greater computer knowledge and proficiency among my employees.")

Moving from Vision to Goals

Your leadership among employees and peers will grow as you lead with a vision. Why? Because most employees want to know where they are going, and they tend to follow an individual who provides clear direction. Once the direction is set, it is critical to outline a strategy to achieve the vision. The implementation of goals plays a significant role in accomplishing any vision.

- List a few reasons why goals might be important for people.

You must fully understand and appreciate the significance of goals in your work environment. When a department or team has a set of well-developed goals, it experiences many benefits. Such goals

- Clarify direction for employees, and communicate what they are doing
- Provide step-by-step organization (strategy)
- Increase people's confidence that the vision can be achieved
- Overcome differences, and focus energy among employees unified for a single mission
- Raise employees' morale when the work process gets close to achieving a goal
- Establish measurements and a track record for future reference
- Greatly influence the workplace culture, and build accountability among the individuals involved

Don't underestimate the power of goals. Make goal setting a normal part of your leadership activities with employees. Use the following guidelines when developing goals.

Guideline 1   Make goals specific. Define each goal, so that it will be clear to everyone what it is that will be achieved.

Guideline 2   Make goals measurable. A goal should be stated in such a way that everyone will know precisely when the goal is achieved.

Guideline 3   Make goals realistic. A goal should be believable and within reach of those who will be striving to achieve it. The resources, tools, and time necessary for the goal to be achieved must be available.

Exercise   Write one goal for your department, following the three guidelines.

Now share your goal statement with your employees. Be open to their suggestions, and then rewrite the statement as needed. Facilitate a meeting in which the department adopts the goal statement. Develop other goals (if necessary).

Moving from Goals to Action Plan

Next, develop an action plan that describes how you will achieve your goal.

Exercise   Using the goal statement you just developed, list the necessary steps to accomplish the goal. Note the order of the steps, the individual(s) involved with each step, the completion date required, and the resources needed to accomplish each step. Use the action plan form in Exhibit 9.1 to record this information.

Making Good Decisions

Part of project management is making the right decision at the right time. There are several techniques and concepts to consider when improving your skills as a wise decision maker:

- Be well informed about the vision and direction of your organization.
- Maintain active goals that are challenging and that reinforce your organization's vision.
- Collect and analyze the most recent and pertinent information.
- Consider the future consequences of any proposed decision; look at both its negative and positive sides.
- Review past decisions that might be similar to your current decision.
- Realize that not everyone will support or understand your decision.
- When possible, involve others (especially employees) in the decision-making process.

There are no secrets to better decision making. Although some supervisors tend to make decisions by the seat of their pants, today there are more reasons than ever to act on the seven ideas just listed. You will greatly improve the decisions you make by taking advantage of the resources available to you. Use them!

Skill #8: Writing Skills

The writing skills addressed in this section will enhance your writing results and also build your confidence about your writing ability. In this section we address a

Action Plan

DEPARTMENT _____ SPONSOR _____

Goal _____

_____

_____

_____

_____

ACTION STEPS	PEOPLE RESPONSIBLE	COMPLETION DATE	RESOURCES NEEDED

Exhibit 9.1. Action Plan

Source: Humphrey and Stokes, *TeamGuides*, p. 39. Copyright © 1997 by Brad Humphrey and Jeff Stokes.

few very common writing efforts that are likely to represent a great percentage of your writing time.

Letter Writing

Take a few minutes to read the following letter. Circle or underline anything that seems incorrect.

> Dear Bill,
>
> I had a grate time meeting with you the other day. I don't think you're company couldn't hardly do better than to start doing business with us. We got the experience and technical knowledge to support our equipment to you satisfaction.
>
> I'll be call you on Wensday to see if you've made a decision yet. Have a good time at Opning Day!
>
> Sincerely,
> *Jack Taylor*

- Describe how you would change this letter:

Guidelines for Better Letter Writing

There is no single correct way to write all letters. You will develop your own style of letter writing that will be appreciated by others. However, there are guidelines that apply to any letter. Incorporate the following guidelines into your letter writing efforts:

Guideline 1 Be clear and concise. Letters are communication without the advantages of voice tone, body language, or immediate two-way conversation as further ways to get your meaning across. Therefore, your letters must be clear and concise, leaving no doubt about what you intend to communicate.

The use of precise names, model numbers, dollar amounts, purchase order numbers, and other details brings clarity to your letter writing. In addition, make sure you do not bury your message in repetitive or unnecessary words. Without being too abrupt, a business letter should come quickly to the point and show respect for the time of the person receiving the letter. The following is an example of a clear, concise letter.

Dear Mrs. Genova:

I just received your returned product: PO# 55332B. A product inspection will be done immediately. You will receive the analysis report by fax as you requested. I fully expect the analysis to be completed within the next five days.

Thank you for bringing this problem to my attention. Our team is committed to maintaining a positive relationship with your firm. This problem will be corrected. I am sorry for any inconvenience this may have caused.

Please contact me if you have any questions. Thank you again for allowing my organization the chance to correct this performance problem.

Sincerely,
Jennifer Jones
Supervisor

Guideline 2   Be positive and upbeat. Even bad news can be presented in a positive way. Emphasizing solutions to any negative information you need to convey in a letter will do much for the way the bad news is received. Analyze the following two statements, and identify which one will encourage the continued business of the customer.

A. We won't be producing your order since our machines will be shut down during our two-week plantwide shut down.

B. We suggest the following three options to meeting your production schedule during our annual two-week plantwide equipment maintenance and safety audit.

Both statements address a two-week period of time when no new products will be manufactured. However, Statement A is blunt, leaving the customer feeling unimportant and without options. Statement B concentrates on what the company can do for the customer.

A letter that reinforces your commitment to a positive result, no matter how negative the situation, communicates to your customers that it is your priority to meet their needs. Don't avoid telling the bad news altogether, but do make all news as positive as possible.

Guideline 3   Be personal and friendly. In most business letters you want to convey a personal and friendly attitude. This guideline is most easily explained through examples, so consider the following two statements and identify which is more personal.

 A. Feel free to sit in on a team meeting and tour our plant facility some time if you are ever in the area.

 B. You are invited to join us for our next team meeting, scheduled for March 13. We would also like to give you a facility tour if you have the time.

The second statement reflects a more personal invitation to the reader and is stated in such a way as to make the reader feel more welcome. Because of the way this invitation is presented, the reader is more likely to accept it than the one in Statement A. To make a letter more personal, concentrate on expressing your interest in the reader and his or her concerns and feelings. Letters that are personal and friendly do much to build strong relationships between the reader and your company.

Guideline 4   Be accurate. Perhaps nothing irritates a reader more than a letter that is laden with obvious factual errors. Any time a percentage, dollar amount, name, date, or any other specific information is used, make sure your source is reliable and that you copy the information correctly. Especially take care to spell the recipient's name correctly. This takes little effort and communicates respect for your reader.

Guideline 5   Express confidence and commitment. It is important to express confidence in your information—and show a commitment to standing by what you say. If you are not sure of your information or what you can do for the reader, research these things before you write the letter. To better understand this potential problem area, read the following statement, and identify how the writer does or does not express confidence and commitment.

 A. I think, at this point, it's possible we might be able to meet your time needs. However, right now we are really busy and are having to move a lot of orders around. If we can't meet your time request I'll try to get back with you about when the real shipping date will be.

The comments in Statement A have the potential to set off all kinds of alarms in the reader's mind about the writer's confidence and commitment level. Even in situations that are not clear, your letter must signal confidence and commitment. Let's rewrite the statement to convey increased confidence and commitment.

B. Your order has been scheduled to be completed by your requested due date of March 17. We will contact you no later than March 11 to confirm that schedule. If we are unable to fill your order by your requested date, we will provide you with a number of alternatives to help you meet your time demands.

The second statement conveys much more confidence and commitment to the customer. If, as in this case, you are not quite sure that a customer's needs can be met, it is wise to let the customer know as soon as possible. However, even if some things are uncertain, it is important to express as much confidence as possible and always show that you are willing to do whatever is necessary to stand behind your word. Remember: managers, fellow supervisors, employees, and customers will accept news better when it is expressed with sincerity, confidence, and a commitment to meeting their needs.

Guideline 6   Double-check letter for errors. Last, but not least, do everything you can to make sure your letters are grammatically correct and free from spelling errors. Many computer programs (almost all word processing programs) have functions that can help you tremendously by checking your grammar and spelling.

A dictionary and a thesaurus are good investments whether or not you have spell checking available to you. If this is a particularly weak area for you, you might also take a basic writing or grammar class at a community college. Finally, always read over your entire letter at least one more time after you finish writing it to check again for grammatical and spelling errors.

Samples of Letters
Use the following samples as models of effective letter writing.

August 28

Ms. Judith N. Gelser
Accurate Health Scales
9834 W. Glenn St.
Haugland, USA

Dear Ms. Gelser:

Thank you for your recent visit to my department to demonstrate your new digital scale. I have had each of my nurses use the scale when taking patient statistics. Thus far the response has been very positive.

I would like you to forward a written sales proposal to me for the Model AA-1 scale. I will include your proposal in my presentation to our hospital administrator next Wednesday, September 3. His positive acceptance of my proposal will allow me to place an order with you for three of the new digital scales, Model AA-1.

Thank you for your assistance. I look forward to making your digital scales part of our total health service.

Best Regards,
Jill Smyth
Nursing Supervisor

July 8

Mr. Todd Coolidge
Purchasing Agent
Towers Electronics Inc.
1212 Nightingale
Crimson Side, USA

Dear Mr. Coolidge:

I felt it was important to update you on the order you placed with us on June 24. As you may recall, I shared with you the information that a strike might take place in July. Unfortunately the strike did begin, at 4:00 P.M. yesterday, July 7.

In spite of the strike, your order will be filled! However, the order will be filled by a different process from the one to which you and I are both accustomed. First, the electronic filters will be supplied by our facility in Farmington. These parts will arrive on July 12, one day past your original due date.

Second, the special chips you ordered will be provided by our Washua facility and are scheduled to be shipped July 9. I expect these parts to be at your location on July 11.

Mr. Coolidge, I am sorry for the inconvenience and hope that my efforts will still help you meet your production schedule. If the arrangements that I have presented do not meet your needs, please call me at your earliest convenience.

Thank you for your business! I look forward to working with you on future orders.

Best Regards,
Bill Tamplin
Supervisor, Shipping and Scheduling Department

Both of these letters are short, clear, and focused on the topic. Notice that both letters go straight to the point of the intended communication. Do not spend a lot of time sweetening up the receiver of your letter, even if the message contained in the letter is negative. Likewise, it is not necessary to share every detail of activity you have experienced, unless the receiver of the letter has asked for such a detailed account.

Exercise   Look at your copies of two or three letters you have written in the past. Using the guidelines presented in this section, critique your letters. Use a red pen or pencil, and make your comments right on the letter. (If you need to keep a clean copy, make additional copies that you can mark up.) After you have assessed your letters, rewrite them, making the noted corrections. As a result of this exercise, you will have your own good models of letters that you can refer to in the future.

One final word about constructing letters. For many supervisors, writing letters, reports, and other messages and documents can be frustrating and cumbersome. We encourage you to hang on and apply the guidelines presented in this last section. With a little practice, you will find that the quality of your writing gets better—and the stress of doing the writing gets less.

Properly constructed letters communicate needed messages and pass along vital information to the recipients. In addition, clearly constructed work instructions are vital to your employees. The next section addresses the format that is most associated with ensuring that employees perform the right work in the right manner.

Standard Operating Procedures

Standard operating procedures (SOPs) assist employees in completing a job more effectively. As the competition and recognition for quality intensify across all industries, SOPs assist you in making every process clear to employees, and reducing the number of mistakes due to simply not understanding a particular job.

SOPs should be organized around four categories: purpose, responsibilities, application, and procedures:

- *Purpose:* The purpose section of a SOP description should clearly express the benefit of putting the procedure into effect. It answers the question, Why are we doing this?

- *Responsibilities:* The responsibilities section describes the roles of all involved individuals or groups and the boundaries for their actions. Specify here who has the responsibility for enforcing accountability, making procedural changes, approving the procedure, and handling document control. This section answers the question, Who is involved?

- *Application:* The application section allows the employee to determine whether the SOP concerns his or her present situation. It answers the question, Where and when does this apply?

- *Procedure:* Finally, we arrive at the heart of the document, answering the question, How should the process be performed? Each process step should be clearly detailed, using terminology that is familiar to the user of the SOP. Operational definitions should be provided for terms with multiple meanings that might be confusing. Rules should be explained. Brevity is preferred. Your objective is to make understanding the description of the procedure as simple as putting on a sweater.

Exhibit 9.2 is an example of an actual standard operating procedure created for conducting performance reviews.

Writing Your Own SOP

Consider a work process within your department that does not have a formal standard operating description. Using the performance review SOP example as a guide and the form in Exhibit 9.3, develop your own SOP. When you finish, present it to your employees for additional insight and support. If your senior manager agrees with your results, adopt the SOP as a formal document to be followed.

Skill #9: Resource Management Skills

Keeping your employees on track and performing at optimum levels will require you to constantly provide needed resources. To make the best resources available to your employees, it will be important for you to use *whom* you know as well as *what* you know.

You need to be in touch with your organization's infrastructure—its people, its resources, and its rules or policies that govern the acquisition of needed resources.

STANDARD OPERATING PROCEDURE

SOP Title: Performance Reviews	
Department: All	**SOP#:** HR-0095
Team: All	**Revision:** 1
Authored by: T.E.G.	**Page:** 1
Approved by: W.H.T.	**Effective Date:** January 25, 1999

I. Purpose

To ensure that each associate is given feedback and coaching on his or her job performance in order to facilitate his or her improvement and increase organizational productivity.

II. Responsibilities

- The associate's immediate supervisor is responsible for gathering feedback on the associate's job performance and presenting the feedback in a one-on-one meeting.
- The director of human resources is responsible for updating and approving this procedure.
- The division managers are responsible for ensuring compliance to this procedure within their respective areas.

III. Application

This procedure applies for all associates.

IV. Procedure

1. The supervisor shall keep a performance log for each associate. Entries are to be made in the log on a monthly, or more frequent, basis. The entries shall indicate recent associate performance in accordance with the evaluation criteria.
2. The supervisor shall obtain at least eight copies of the associate performance evaluation form and distribute them to the associate's internal customers, direct reports, and other peers. These individuals should return the completed forms to the supervisor one week prior to the scheduled performance review.
3. The supervisor averages the observer scores and writes them on the official performance review sheet, which will be shared with the associate and kept on file in the Human Resources Department.
4. The supervisor reviews the log and determines how he or she desires to score the associate's performance.
5. The supervisor records his or her score on the official feedback form.
6. The supervisor notifies the associate of the time and date of the performance review meeting. One hour should be allocated for the meeting.
7. The supervisor shall not take any telephone calls or answer any pages during the feedback session.
8. The supervisor should stress that the presented feedback is the accumulation of input from several people, including other associates and internal customers.
9. The supervisor should hand the associate the written feedback form and give the associate adequate time to read it.
10. Together the supervisor and the associate should address each feedback item, discussing what outstanding performance would be for each item and why the associate's scores might have been what they were.
11. At the end of the meeting the associate signs and dates the bottom of the form indicating the information was presented and discussed. Signing does not indicate associate agreement with the actual scores.
12. If the meeting needs to run longer than one hour, the associate and the supervisor shall set a time and date for a continuation of the meeting. The follow-up should take place within one week from the original meeting.
13. The supervisor keeps a copy of the feedback form locked up in his or her office and forwards the official copy to the Human Resources Department.

Exhibit 9.2. Standard Operating Procedure

STANDARD OPERATING PROCEDURE

SOP Title:	
Department:	SOP#:
Team:	Revision:
Authored by:	Page:
Approved by:	Effective Date:

I. Purpose

II. Responsibilities

III. Application

IV. Procedure

Exhibit 9.3. Standard Operating Procedure

Exercise   Consider the types of resources you may need to secure for your employees. For each type of resource listed in the left-hand column, write in the right-hand column an actual example of the resource as it is required in your department.

Resource   *Example*

Tools

Cost information

Software

Supplier information

Company expectations

An assistant

Time

Equipment upgrade

Training

Books, manuals, and so forth

Computer support

Customer needs

Completing the previous exercise should enable you to achieve a better idea of what your employees need to do their jobs. As you work on this exercise, you may want to discuss job needs with your employees.

Your next effort should be to identify when the resources will be needed. This allows you to have the resources available as they need to be used.

The benefit of having this type of information recorded and accessible is that it reduces the guesswork you might otherwise have to do to anticipate the needs of others. This is especially important when you must develop and maintain a budget for all of the resources and expenses in your work area.

Identifying the resource needs of your department provides the information you will need when networking with others. Networking is addressed in the next section. It strongly supports your efforts to make needed resources available to your workforce.

Networking

Networking is nothing more than the process of meeting people who can help you meet the resource needs of your employees. Networking can take place in almost any environment.

- List your normal environments in which you might meet someone who could provide a needed resource for you or your employees.

The following techniques can improve your networking skills.

- When you meet someone, secure his or her name, company name, telephone number, and e-mail and mailing addresses. (A business card normally holds all this information.)

- When you meet people, ask what line of work or industry they are in. Ask how they perform their work, and how much experience they have.

- Make or obtain your own business cards, and hand them out to new contacts.

- Attend industry-related conferences, seminars, trade shows, and so on.

- Request information and assistance on using the Internet as a resource (surfing the Net).
- Call authors of books and magazine articles to secure additional information.
- When attending conferences, offer to take the speaker to lunch or dinner.
- Introduce yourself to suppliers, and ask for the names of their inside support people.
- When you learn that new equipment or technology is available, ask if you can send some of your employees to learn how to operate the equipment or technology.
- Be quick to ask questions; don't be a know-it-all. (Play dumb periodically.)
- Accept people as they are, and never overlook the knowledge or experience they might be able to share with you.

You will find many opportunities presented to you to acquire more information, expertise, and resources as you learn to network. Using the suggestions just presented will help you to create new friendships with other experts from different fields of specialty.

Networking plays off the old saying, "It's not what you know but who you know." Truly, the many different individuals you know may have keys to new and better experiences for you and the people who work for you.

The final resource management skill that we address is learning how to create a budget. Think back to the earlier discussion about securing resources as you read this section. As you continue to grow as a professional supervisor, it will become increasingly important for you to be able to create a budget and use it to manage your resources.

Creating a Budget

Developing and maintaining a budget requires you to be financially alert and educated. Having a working knowledge of the budget for your department will help you (1) make effective and smart business decisions, (2) improve your allocation of resources, and (3) remain current on needed supplies for your employees and the cost of supplies expended.

There are several techniques for developing an accurate budget. Review the five components of budget development before creating your budget.

Budget Components

- Current expenses for performing the necessary work (expenses for materials, supplies, support, labor rates, preventive maintenance, tools, equipment, and so forth)
- Three-year history of expenses and average yearly increases or decreases
- Projected increases of work to be achieved
- Projected increases in expenses to support projected increased performance
- Time period covered by the budget

To secure this information you will need to contact senior leaders. Where expenses of supplies or hourly rates are involved, your financial department should assist you by securing the information.

The following exercise and its accompanying budget form detail many items that may be important to include in your budget. Feel free to add items before you compile your budget for the next calendar year. If this is your first effort to develop a budget, present it to your senior leader for his or her feedback.

Exercise Begin work on developing a one-year budget. For each item that applies to you listed in the left-hand column, record in the right-hand column the projected budget expense. Be sure to add additional items that also apply, along with their projected expenses. You may need to break some single items into multiple items to accurately reflect the projected costs.

Budget Items	*Projected Budget Expense*
Labor	
Overtime	
Outside consultants	
Training	

Budget Items	*Projected Budget Expense*
New equipment, tools, and so forth	
Equipment maintenance	
Material needs (paper, files, raw material for production, and so forth)	
Incentives or bonuses	
Supplies	
Travel costs	
Subscriptions, association dues	
Recognition awards	
Department socials	

Administrative Skills in Review

The administrative side of supervision is sometimes known as the ugly side of leadership. Most of the administrative skills you need require behind-the-scenes effort. All three administrative skill areas that we discuss here require your dedication to ensuring that information is secured, analyzed, processed, and passed on in the most effective and user-friendly manner. Administrative skills are the third leg of the three-legged skills stool. If you do not develop your administrative skills fully, you will never quite achieve the solid base from which you can lead others.

In your never-ending process to be the best supervisor possible, don't be surprised if you grow impatient with the administrative side of leadership. Much administrative work is underappreciated and goes unrecognized—until a project is not completed on time or a letter to a customer is not written or there is no money left in the budget because no one carefully considered increasing the budget in light of the work to be done and the resources needed.

The best form of recognition you may ever receive will come when your employees no longer complain about shortages of materials, tools, information, or money. Work hard to develop your administrative skills, and you will separate yourself from other supervisors—and find yourself in full view of senior leaders who appreciate your work and can influence your future rise in status and financial success.

Chapter 10

• •

Developing Your
Personal Improvement Plan

Assessing your supervisory skills is only the first step toward becoming a more effective leader at the front lines. It is important for your professional growth as a supervisor that you select a path to better leadership and performance.

The Personal Improvement Plan (PIP) will bring greater direction to your future as a supervisor. The PIP is your personal road map to improving the skills assessed by the Supervisor 360° Skill Assessment. You will also work with a manager (preferably your immediate manager) who will support your improvement effort.

What the PIP Can Do for You

- Allow you to keep your long-term future and short-term future in perspective
- Focus your attention on the specific improvement steps you need to take
- Identify specific dates for action steps to be completed
- Tie your immediate skill needs to future job aspiration
- Involve a manager who will provide objective support

The Personal Improvement Plan is a tool that allows you to objectively address what you need to do to improve your supervisory skills. The PIP will be your action plan for making the needed improvements. It will provide a system of accountability to ensure greater support for your improvement success.

Exhibit 10.1 is a form for your Personal Improvement Plan. Complete as much of the PIP now as possible. Use the additional instructions provided in the text for each section. Complete these steps in the text of this chapter before seeking a manager to support your efforts.

• •

PERSONAL IMPROVEMENT PLAN

Name _____ Job Title _____

Length of Employment _____ Tenure in Current Job _____

Date _____

The Personal Improvement Plan (PIP) helps you map out your career development and skill improvement.

CAREER DIRECTION

1. Describe your current job tasks, responsibilities, and skills. Be as detailed as possible.

2. Which three skill areas assessed by your S-360 received the lowest average scores?

3. What skills do you have that you feel are underutilized?

4. What additional training and resources do you need for your current job?

5. Describe the next position you would like to fill in your organization.

6. How will your efforts to achieve your next desired position be supported by improving the three skill areas in which you received your lowest scores?

Exhibit 10.1. Personal Improvement Plan

ACTION PLAN (CURRENT YEAR)

Design a plan of action for your skill development. Your plan should describe the action you need to take, when the action will be taken, your manager's contribution toward ensuring the action steps are completed, and the completion date. Choose one of the nine skill areas in which you received the lowest score. (You may plan to improve more than one skill with this PIP. However, it is often most effective to focus on one skill at a time.)

The skill area I selected is _____

Description of Action	When Action Is to Be Taken	Manager Action	Completion Date

Exhibit 10.1. continued.

LONG-TERM CAREER DIRECTION

1. What position and responsibilities do you aspire to attain in three years?

2. What position and responsibilities do you aspire to attain in five years?

3. Hcw will the improvement of your selected skill area support your long-term aspirations?

4. Describe how you will know when you have made improvement in your selected skill area.

Commitment to improve signature (self) _____

Commitment to support signature (manager) _____

Exhibit 10.1. continued.

Completing the PIP

The following instructions will assist you in completing the PIP, item by item.

Personal Improvement Plan

Name. Give your name.

Length of employment. State how long (years/months) you have worked for your present organization.

Job title. State your official job title.

Tenure in current job. State how long (years/months) you have held your present job title.

Date. Enter the date you complete the PIP and begin to work on the improvement steps.

Career Direction

1. *Describe your current job tasks, responsibilities, and skills*. Be as detailed as possible. Be thorough and clear. You may use abbreviations. If necessary, attach additional paper to this PIP to list all needed information about your current work.

2. *Which three skill areas assessed by your S-360 received the lowest average scores?* Review your S-360 results, and list the three skills that received the lowest average observer scores.

3. *What skills do you have that you feel are underutilized?* Are there skills that you believe you possess but are not able to use in your current job function? Describe these skills, and state why you are unable to use them.

4. *What additional training and resources do you need for your current job?* For example, do you need training in computers, problem solving, or making a presentation? And what resources do you need to make these needed improvements (for example, time, tuition for a local college class, personal coach or mentor, access to more information)? Describe what you need and why.

5. *Describe the next position you would like to fill in your organization*. Describe this job by title and function. Briefly explain why you want this job and why you believe you can fulfill the tasks and responsibilities of this job.

6. *How will your efforts to achieve your next desired position be supported by improving the three skill areas in which you received your lowest scores?* Describe how specific improvements in the three skill areas where you received the lowest average observer scores would enable you to successfully carry out the job function you identified in item 5.

Action Plan (Current Year)

This section asks you to complete four components for each item in your action plan. The first component, the description of an improvement action, should be completed first. The next three components will be filled out accordingly.

Description of action. Name each step you will take to improve your identified skill. You may find that some action steps cannot be started or completed until others are achieved. If this is the case, prioritize the action items. This will keep you more organized, focused, and on schedule.

When action is to be taken. Record the dates by which you intend to complete each step.

Manager action. It is possible to make these improvements without a manager's support, but it is better and wiser to have a manager act as your sponsor to assist your efforts. This manager should be familiar with you and your need for skill improvement and be willing to take the time to encourage you and hold you accountable. Complete this section with the manager present, so you can agree on the actions he or she must take to assist you with a step.

Completion date. The date the action item is actually completed.

Long-Term Career Direction

This final section of the Personal Improvement Plan focuses on the job roles you would like to achieve in three years and in five years. Your aspirations may change periodically as you grow in your job; however, this section challenges you to think about where you would like your career to head in the future. It is also important to consider the relationship between your long-term aspirations and your skill improvements.

1. *What position and responsibilities do you aspire to attain in three years?* (See the instructions for the next question.)

2. *What position and responsibilities do you aspire to attain in five years?* These two questions require you to consider the career direction you would like to take. State the actual job title of the position you desire in each instance. If your aspirations are focused more on expanding your skill and knowledge base than on a specific job, describe the skills or knowledge you desire to obtain.

3. *How will the improvement of your selected skill area support your long-term aspirations?* It is critical to evaluate the relationship between where you hope to be and the skills that will lead you to that point. Address the skills you need to improve your current performance first. Then begin work on the skills you will need in the future.

4. *Describe how you will know when you have made improvement in your selected skill area.* Like goal setting, determining a measurable end result provides a target and confirms your achievement of the desired result. You might know you have improved if you see an increase in the average observer scores on your S-360 in six to twelve months, if you get positive feedback from your manager and your peers, if you experience greater ease in exercising the particular skill, and so forth.

Commitment to improve signature (self). Sign your name only if you are serious about improving the skill area addressed in this PIP.

Commitment to support signature (manager). The manager should understand that by signing the PIP he or she is committing to take the time necessary to encourage you and hold you accountable.

Enhancing Your Career with the PIP

The strength of the Personal Improvement Plan is that it serves as a constant reminder of the direction you desire for your career and also defines the skills you will need. The completed PIP will reinforce your commitment to be at your best and to stay focused.

Making improvements in your skill development is a straightforward process. The first step is to recognize the areas that need improvement. By completing the Supervisor 360° Skill Assessment, you initiated this process. The next step is to identify the skill areas in greatest need of improvement and to design a plan to improve those skills. The Personal Improvement Plan supports this effort by providing you with a road map for your own personal improvement strategy.

The next section of this chapter examines how you can build greater accountability into your improvement process. Although you may start off with a sincere desire to improve, daily pressures will pull and tug for your attention. This may take your focus away from improvement opportunities and prevent you from making the time to work on the needed skills.

Building Accountability into Your PIP

You must make a personal effort to improve your skills in order to succeed in becoming a more effective supervisor. Accountability is, first and foremost, a personal issue! If you are committed to making the needed improvements in your supervisory skills, you will find most people to be positive and supportive.

Although your own mental attitude is important, several specific actions can build greater accountability into your effort to improve your supervisory skill areas. The following actions will contribute to keeping you focused, motivated, and accountable.

- Select a sponsoring manager who knows you and is not afraid to provide honest, objective feedback.

- Once you and your manager have signed the PIP, make sure both you and your manager get a copy of it.

- Schedule monthly meetings with your manager to discuss your progress in raising your skill(s) and to go over any questions or difficulty you may be experiencing.

- Set personal rewards for yourself when you complete specific action steps on your PIP. (This will reinforce your hard work.)

- Have the S-360 redone in six to twelve months. Compare your new results against those you received previously. With your manager, identify improvements that you have achieved. Update your PIP, and continue your effort to improve needed skill areas.

- Determine that you want to improve and that nothing is going to stop you.

Do not become frustrated in your skill development. You will find that some skill development efforts are easier than others. You may need to spend additional time on some skill areas, whereas other skills will develop quickly. Also, keep in mind that becoming more knowledgeable about a skill is not the same as performing the skill with confidence. Confidence may arrive more slowly. Be patient with your efforts—you will be successful!

Suggested Resources

· ·

The Supervisor 360° Skill Assessment and *The 21st Century Supervisor Participant Workbook* are designed to be used in conjunction with *The 21st Century Supervisor: Nine Essential Skills for Frontline Leaders*. *The 21st Century Supervisor* provides a complete, thorough explanation of the importance of the nine skills diagnosed in the assessment, how supervisors can apply them, and the skill assessment instrument. If you would like to further explore some of the topics, we recommend the following resources.

People Skills

Communication Skills

Burley-Allen, M. *Listening: The Forgotten Skill*. New York: Wiley, 1995.

Editors of Career Press. *Powerful Presentation Skills: A Quick and Handy Guide for Any Manager or Business Owner*. Hawthorne, N.J.: Career Press, 1993.

Humphrey, B., and Stokes, J. *InterSpective Communications: Appreciating Diverse Personalities*. Shawnee, Kans.: Pinnacle Performance Group, 1999.

Team Skills

Humphrey, B., and Stokes, J. *TeamGuides: A Self-Directed System for Teams*. San Francisco: Jossey-Bass/Pfeiffer, 1997.

Rees, F. *How to Lead Work Teams: Facilitation Skills*. San Francisco: Jossey-Bass/Pfeiffer, 1991.

Scholtes, P. R., Joiner, B.L., and Streibel, B. J. *The Team Handbook: How to Use Teams to Improve Quality*. Madison, Wis.: Oriel, 1996.

Wilson, J. M., George, J., Wellins, R. S., and Byham, W. C., *Leadership Trapeze: Strategies for Leadership in Team-Based Organizations*. San Francisco: Jossey-Bass, 1994.

Coaching Skills

Bacal, R. *Performance Management*. New York: McGraw-Hill, 1998.

· ·

Hargrove, R. *Masterful Coaching: Extraordinary Results by Impacting People and the Way They Think and Work Together.* San Francisco: Jossey-Bass/Pfeiffer, 1995.

Whitmore, J. *Coaching for Performance (People Skills for Professionals).* (2nd ed.) Sonoma, Calif.: Brealey, 1996.

Technical Skills

Business Analysis Skills

Kaplan, R. S., and Cooper, R. *Cost and Effect: Using Integrated Cost Systems to Drive Profitability and Performance.* Boston: Harvard Business School Press, 1998.

Miller, J. A. *Implementing Activity-Based Management in Daily Operations.* New York: Wiley, 1995.

Monden, Y. *Cost Management in the New Manufacturing Age: Innovations in the Japanese Automotive Industry.* Cambridge, Mass.: Productivity Press, 1992.

Continuous Improvement Skills

Chang, R. Y. *Continuous Process Improvement: A Practical Guide to Improving Processes for Measurable Results.* Irvine, Calif.: Chang Associates, 1994.

Kepner, C. H., and Tregoe, B. B. *The New Rational Manager.* Princeton, N.J.: Princeton Research Press, 1981.

Robinson, A. *Continuous Improvement in Operations: A Systematic Approach to Waste Reduction.* Cambridge, MA: Productivity Press, 1993.

Sashkin, M., and Kiser, K. J. *Putting Total Quality Management to Work: What TQM Means, How to Use It and How to Sustain It over the Long Run.* San Francisco: Berrett-Koehler, 1993.

Computer Skills

Family members, friends, coworkers, and yourself. The best and easiest method for learning how to use computers and software is to get someone else's help. Personal trial and error is the most common approach to learning computer software.

Your local community college. Most community colleges offer classes in learning how to run computers and work with various software packages. Many classes meet one or two nights a week for only four to six weeks or meet over a weekend, beginning on Friday and ending on Saturday.

Training videos. Computer training videocassettes can be purchased from mail-order companies and many bookstores, rented from video stores, and borrowed from public libraries. They are an excellent learning tool if you have access to a computer.

Administrative Skills

Project Management Skills

Rouillard, L. A. *Goals and Goal Setting.* Los Altos, Calif.: Crisp, 1998.

Thomsett, M. C. *The Little Black Book of Project Management.* New York: AMACOM, 1990.

Wysocki, R. K., and Weiss, J. (eds.). *Five-Phase Project Management: A Practical Planning and Implementation Guide*. Reading, Mass.: Perseus Press, 1992.

Writing Skills

Fine, E. H., and Josephson, J. P. *Nitty-Gritty Grammar, A Not-So-Serious Guide to Clear Communication*. Berkeley, Calif.: Ten Speed Press, 1998.

Muckian, M., and Woods, J. *The Business Letter Handbook: How to Write Effective Letters and Memos for Every Business Situation*. Holbrook, Mass.: Adams Media, 1996.

Toropov, B. *Sixty Second Memos*. Upper Saddle River, N.J.: Prentice Hall, 1997.

Resource Management Skills

Axelrod, A., Holtje, J., and Holtje, J. *201 Ways to Manage Your Time Better*. New York: McGraw-Hill, 1997.

Finney, R. G. *Essentials of Business Budgeting*. New York: AMACOM, 1995.

Goldratt, E. M., and Cox, J. *The Goal: A Process of Ongoing Improvement*. New York: North River Press, 1994.

Valuable Books on Leadership

Belasco, J. A., and Staver, R. C. *Flight of the Buffalo: Soaring to Excellence, Learning to Let Employees Lead*. New York: Warner Books, 1994.

Blanchard, K. *Leadership and the One Minute Manager*. San Francisco: Jossey-Bass, 1996.

Blanchard, K., and Johnson, S. *The One Minute Manager*. San Francisco: Jossey-Bass, 1997.

Byham, W. C., and Cox, J. *Zapp! The Lightning of Empowerment: How to Improve Productivity, Quality, and Employee Satisfaction*. New York: Ballantine, 1998.

Kouzes, J. M., and Posner, B. Z. *The Leadership Challenge: How to Get Extraordinary Things Done in Organizations*. San Francisco: Jossey-Bass, 1996.